BEHAVIOR
BREAKTHROUGH

BEHAVIOR

BREAKTHROUGH

TWELVE SKILLS TO TRANSFORM BEHAVIOR AT HOME AND IN THE CLASSROOM

Bailey Payne, BCBA *with* Jen Lill Brown

NEW YORK

LONDON • NASHVILLE • MELBOURNE • VANCOUVER

Behavior Breakthrough

12 Skills to Transform Behavior at Home and in the Classroom

Published in New York, New York, by Morgan James Publishing. Morgan James is a trademark of Morgan James, LLC. www.MorganJamesPublishing.com

Proudly distributed by Publishers Group West®

Morgan James BOGO™

A **FREE** ebook edition is available for you or a friend with the purchase of this print book.

CLEARLY SIGN YOUR NAME ABOVE

Instructions to claim your free ebook edition:
1. Visit MorganJamesBOGO.com
2. Sign your name CLEARLY in the space above
3. Complete the form and submit a photo of this entire page
4. You or your friend can download the ebook to your preferred device

ISBN 9781636984933 paperback
ISBN 9781636984940 ebook
Library of Congress Control Number:
2024936535

Cover and Interior Design by:
Ian Koviak

Morgan James is a proud partner of Habitat for Humanity Peninsula and Greater Williamsburg. Partners in building since 2006.

Get involved today! Visit: www.morgan-james-publishing.com/giving-back

DEDICATION

This book is a testament to God's grace and second
chances bestowed upon us. Our journey, marked by a newfound
freedom and hope in the gift of salvation, is grounded in our
unwavering faith and love for Jesus Christ, providing us
with a solid foundation to share our story.

TABLE OF CONTENTS

Y ou'll notice some subtle nods to fairy tales in this book. Why?

First, because happy endings to stories make everyone feel good. But second, and more importantly, because when you focus on the data and remain consistent, you'll truly feel like you have defeated the darkness and found the keys to brighter days ahead.

And can't we all agree that the best stories are not when a knight in shining armor saves the day but when the hero or heroine realizes they had the power within them all along to find their breakthrough!

I want you to know that the power to affect behavioral change is in your hands. So, turn the page, and let's get started.

PART I

STRONG FOUNDATIONS LEAD TO HAPPY ENDINGS

Embarking on a journey into new territory within any subject can feel overwhelming, especially if you feel desperate for things to change. But fear not—even the most complex situations can become manageable with the right approach.

Part I sets the stage for a happy ending, where you become a master of reinforcement who is skilled at increasing desired behaviors. There are a lot of misconceptions about reinforcement, so we'll set the record straight and help you understand the term.

As a behavior analyst who is passionate about sparking change, my goal is to prepare you for a successful journey so you can start using these behavioral skills (I also refer to them as "strategies") to create real and lasting change.

It doesn't matter where you are or what challenges you face; you can create an environment where reinforcement and instructional control are the norm, bringing with them peace, success, and happier days for all.

As a mother of two strong-willed girls who embrace every fairy tale to the fullest, I have watched my girls feel overwhelming fear as each hero or heroine battles the evil power. But I have also watched my girls sparkle with hope as each hero is victorious with a bit of perseverance and bravery.

CHAPTER 1

Hope Isn't Just For Fairy Tales

nce upon a time, there lived a group of parents and educators in the town of Brightville who faced a predicament. Their loved ones and students, blessed with marvelous potential, found themselves entangled in a web of undesirable behavior that hindered their growth and happiness.

As the days passed, frustration spread like a dark cloud over Brightville, casting its shadow over the homes and classrooms. Desperation seeped into the hearts of the townspeople, for they longed to see their loved ones flourish.

But hope loomed on the horizon when a mysterious stranger, Mrs. Emerson, arrived in town. Mrs. Emerson firmly believed everyone deserved the opportunity to thrive regardless of age or circumstance. She understood that the key to unlocking their boundless potential lay within the realm of reinforcement and environmental control.

Mrs. Emerson embarked on a quest to bring about transformation in the lives of those around her. But she knew that in order to change how loved ones and learners behaved, a change must first occur within the hearts and minds of those who guided them.

With great determination, Mrs. Emerson began to teach the people of Brightville how to reshape others with empathy and changes in their environmental interactions. She awakened the hearts of parents and educators alike with the immense power of reinforcement. She showed them how small gestures displayed encouragement and love, which inspired their loved ones to unravel their truest, brightest selves.

The townspeople gathered around Mrs. Emerson. They wanted to learn her secrets, to grasp the transformative power she possessed. And so, armed with the proper behavioral strategy tools, they embarked on a journey of personal growth and self-discovery.

As the days turned into weeks, a remarkable change took hold. The once chaotic homes and classrooms blossomed into havens of joy and tranquility. Laughter and harmony filled the air, replacing the heavy frustration as the townspeople experienced behavior breakthroughs.

The people of Brightville flourished like flowers in a sunlit meadow. Challenging behaviors slowly faded, giving rise to a thirst for knowledge and a desire to be kinder to others. They embraced the lessons of empathy and understanding, nurturing bonds of unity, and lived happily ever after.

The tale of Brightville's transformation speaks to the power of love and reinforcement. It teaches us that, much like in our childhood fairy tales, even the greatest challenges can be overcome with an open heart and the right tools.

You will embark on a transformative journey through these pages—with me as your guide. Like Mrs. Emerson, I know every person around you deserves the chance to show you just how amazing they are. I want to help you learn the art of instructional control and environmental contingencies and discover the delicate balance between structure and flexibility that allows everyone to be their best.

One thing you and I have in common is this: we want to live in an environment of growth and harmony. But sometimes, challenging or undesired behaviors can make it seem our best efforts aren't enough or correct.

That is where tangible behavioral skills come into play—practical strategies that can transform chaos into order, frustration into cooperation, and resistance into engagement.

With each new skill, you will witness the rewarding moments when challenging behaviors begin to melt away, replaced by cooperation and confidence. The goal is to help you provide reinforcement and thereby see your child's or learner's behavior improve. Ultimately, what you will experience is a behavior breakthrough:

BEHAVIOR BREAKTHROUGH

A transformative moment marked by a significant desired change in actions and attitudes. It's achieved by applying proven methods that encourage prosocial behavior and empower those around you to control their surroundings effectively. This breakthrough signifies a noticeable rise in desired behaviors, fostering a sense of accomplishment and optimism. It's a journey driven by practical strategies and data that promotes personal growth and inspires beneficial change.

This book invites you to embrace a new way of relating to the unique humans in your care. Whether you are a parent seeking harmony at home or a teacher striving to create an oasis of learning, you now hold the keys to a world where reinforcement delivery reigns supreme.

Using evidence-based approaches, you can create conditions anywhere that promote the behaviors you wish to see and ultimately enhance learning outcomes. The power to transform lies within each of us—and on these pages, you will find the guidance to unlock it.

CONTROL ISN'T A FOUR-LETTER WORD

Are you looking for a path to learn new skills quickly and create an environment based on instructional control that brings out the absolute best in those around you? Then you found the right resource! But why would you want to increase "instructional control" in the first place?

Instructional control is the key to creating the motivation to follow your lead and do more of what produces the best outcomes for everyone.

Rather than delivering threats, you can grow satisfying, mutually respectful relationships. As a result, others will know that listening to you leads to rewards while avoiding adverse outcomes. Once you establish instructional control, your presence is more valuable to the child or learner.

I know the word "control" gets a bad rap, but it isn't bad—it's *necessary*. Controlling an environment increases behavioral predictability, safety, and overall trust. And right now, if you're like most people, you recognize times when you feel squarely out of control in your professional or personal life. That feeling of being out of control results from the absence of predictability in interactions, leading to desperation and hopelessness.

I'm telling you, there's hope.

That hope rests in you experiencing a Behavior Breakthrough. It's possible when you are committed to increasing the behaviors you want to see in others and decreasing the ones that steal joy and potential. As you read this book and apply the behavioral skills, the goal is for you to experience:

1. A noticeable increase in joy and harmony.
2. A less hectic pace, thanks to a mutual desire to avoid problem behaviors.
3. A lifestyle change that will help you become more fluent in using reinforcement effectively.

I designed this book to be read easily, but it's not a quick fix. However, if you are reading these pages, I know you are not looking for an easy way to pass the blame. So, stick with me, and I will deliver proven skills to increase desired behavior. The behavioral skills in this book are not the same ones our society or instincts tell us to use; they require conscious effort to implement.

With a bit of reinforcement, you can adjust your behavior and responses. At the same time, you will see the behavior of various people change; they will learn to interact with you and others appropriately.

You are deeply invested in creating behavior change, or you wouldn't be here. And that's the only foundation we need to make this work. So, consider yourself one giant leap closer to success already. Ultimately, it's about changing *you* and your responses, which has a ripple effect on those around you.

A MISSION BORNE OUT OF DARKNESS

The aha moment for this book came at the darkest time of my life.

I faced the same reality that many people faced during the 2020 pandemic. The whole world shut down, and those of us who make our living meeting face-to-face with people wondered if life would ever look the same again. For me, the pandemic threatened my entire livelihood. I couldn't offer in-person therapy or enter a school or patient's home.

But that didn't stop the calls. I was receiving cries from parents desperate for behavioral help because challenging behaviors were at an all-time high. There seemed to be no relief in sight.

Ironically, I was crying out for help, too. At that point, I was a single mom (I've since remarried), and the lockdown was devastating for me. I could no longer send my child to daycare and was left to counsel struggling and desperate caregivers virtually with a toddler at my feet around the clock.

One night in late March 2020, I was at the end of my rope. I decided to start a Facebook page to reach parents and provide behavioral strategies to increase overall mental health and happiness. I wanted to create an avenue to dispense behavioral tips to feel like I was doing something, anything, to help others stuck at home, increase instructional control, and decrease challenging behaviors.

The Facebook page allowed me to reach many people at once instead of logging onto virtual one-on-one sessions all day with a rambunctious toddler in the background. I connected with like-minded people; in the process, I benefited from my own professional advice, especially since I was not only a behavior analyst but also a parent.

I started getting private messages that let me know the information resonated with my growing audience. The posts were making an impact, so I continued. I felt blessed to be able to help in any way I could. That planted the seed that I could turn this thing into a movement to provide more profound assistance to more people.

And now here we are.

The pandemic is over, but the damage from that time remains for many. Millions of children and their parents and educators now find themselves dealing with the long-term repercussions of:

1. **Social isolation:** Lack of peer contact and limited face-to-face interactions impacted emotional and social development. We'll feel the ripple effects for years.

2. **Disrupted routines:** When routines are disrupted, people feel stress and anxiety. They have difficulty adjusting to new schedules. These challenges can lead to behavioral issues.

3. **Increased screen time:** Screen time exploded during the pandemic and hasn't decreased as much as we'd hoped. Excessive screen time has been associated with sleep disturbances, reduced physical activity, attention difficulties, and decreased academic performance.

4. **Anxiety and stress:** Concerns about personal health, the health of loved ones, and the disruption of their lives led many children to act out. Their behavioral changes manifested in irritability, mood swings, and difficulty concentrating.

5. **Reduced physical activity:** Lockdown measures limited children's opportunities for physical activity and outdoor play since parents were working from home and unable to take them outside. That negatively affected physical health, contributing to obesity, decreased fitness levels, and reduced overall well-being.

6. **Emotional distress:** The pandemic introduced children to new stressors that led to emotional distress, including symptoms of depression, anxiety, or behaviorally-related disorders, such as oppositional defiance disorder, disruptive behavior disorder, and conduct disorder.

7. **Learning difficulties:** The transition back and forth to remote learning posed challenges for many children, particularly those from disadvantaged backgrounds or with limited access to resources.

These issues were added to the existing challenges that millions of people faced. Many were already dealing with various challenges like divorce, abuse, family relocations, or crowded households. Many more dealt with issues surrounding neurological functioning, which stemmed from a disorder, syndrome, or deficiency. Or they simply have a strong-willed personality or pre-existing barriers in homes that led to increased difficulties during the pandemic.

There is almost no end to the causes of behavior changes or struggles—and over the years, I've seen it all. I have worked with children, teens, and adults in group homes, state hospitals, schools, homes, communities, clinics, and as a direct therapist. I have worked with child protective services and the foster care system and with those suffering under the weight of poverty, unable to access services.

I'm also keenly familiar with living in a rural area where accessing services is challenging and *quality* services are almost nonexistent. I work with people with neurological diagnoses whose brains function differently—those with one, two, or more diagnoses (as well as those who may be struggling but have not met diagnostic criteria). I have also parented as a single mom at one point in my life, so I understand the nuanced challenges of traveling this road alone with limited resources or barriers out of your control.

In these diverse environments, I have witnessed the principles of applied behavioral analysis become the foundation for visible change. No matter the barrier, I regularly watch these readily available, easy-to-implement behavioral skills prove to be beneficial and highly impactful.

As a professional and parent, it's my job to evaluate the behavior around me, my own behavior, and all environmental variables present. I've had significant losses and had to pick myself up by the bootstraps with minimal support. While I recognize the advantages of my background, education, employment, transportation, and ethnicity, I'm not immune to walking lonely, dark roads where desperation is the primary driving force.

I'm here today and able to deliver these tangible strategies because of the love and grace of Jesus Christ and my passion for staying rooted in the principles of applied behavioral analysis. After all, these skills made my once dark and lonely road doable. It's only fitting to pass along the lifeline.

It is unrealistic to say, "Do these steps and never have behavior challenges again." But there are ways to vastly and tangibly improve. Often, behavioral change occurs in small steps, but each step provides momentum to climb toward profound change. The minor daily improvements add up and radically transform overall behavior, attitude, and outlook on life.

Minor daily improvements can be motivating, and with this continued momentum, revolutionary changes occur in your environment that are total game-changers. Will challenging behaviors still happen? Of course! All children (and adults, for that matter) have inappropriate behaviors from time to time. I get angry, I get frustrated, and I run out of patience. Those are all normal.

But just because it's "normal" doesn't mean we must accept a response as the default.

The way to change those defaults? To fix the language surrounding challenging or undesirable behaviors. And that starts with you, the adult. How do you react to a negative outcome in your own life? What behaviors are you modeling for those around you? That is part of the bigger picture and why I always tell my patients' parents that this journey will change everyone, not just their child.

And that's a good thing! Who doesn't want to become a better spouse, co-worker, boss, relative, or friend?

TRUST THE SCIENCE (NO, REALLY)

Chances are, this book isn't your first attempt at learning how to change the behaviors you're experiencing. Maybe you follow a blog, have read other books, or even signed up for a course. Your child or a student could be meeting with a therapist.

Maybe some of it has worked (at least briefly).

Maybe you feel like you're spinning your wheels.

I want to help you unstick the wheels, gain traction, and fill your hope tank.

Some children are fortunate to have access to behavioral therapy, but let's be honest—there are many barriers to accessing behavioral treatment. You must receive a formal diagnosis, have some type of insurance or funding program, and live in an area where the services are available.

If you are lucky enough to have access to services, what is the quality of those offerings?

If you can access exceptional services, you may learn functional skills that improve social awareness, problem-solving, communication, and daily living. You may develop more tolerance or independence. You may see challenging behaviors decrease. Yet, even top-notch services are limited. How many hours a week will your child actually be in a counseling session?

At most, you have multiple hours a week. But it's more like maybe an hour a week of therapy.

The lion's share of the work will always fall to the caregiver or teacher who spends the most face time with the child or children. That's why those services aim to *introduce* you to effective strategies but not *instill* them. That's on you.

I plan to bridge that gap—to deliver the needed approaches in a format that will help YOU internalize them.

The techniques will feel deliberate initially, but that's because they are new. They will initially sound foreign to your loved ones and students. After a while, they will become more like muscle memory, carried out with minimal thought and effort. They will become engrained in your language and in who you are.

Experiencing a Behavior Breakthrough means you're becoming a contingency expert in all areas of life. We're talking about improving your interactions with your spouse, family, coworkers, supervisors, customers, and more through instructional control and evidence-based strategies. **While most examples will be geared toward children (young to teen), these scientifically proven behavioral skills are impactful despite age, diagnosis, socioeconomic class, or any other identifying characteristic.**

The beauty of science-backed strategies is they aren't anecdotal. Regarding behavioral skills, "anecdotal" means information based on personal stories and observations rather than scientific research. It's all about people sharing their experiences and what has worked for them in dealing with behavior issues.

But anecdotal evidence has its limits. It's not the same as scientific data or a guarantee that something will work for everyone. It's based on personal stories and perspectives, so you must take this type of evidence with a grain of salt.

Doing what another parent did because it worked for them is like going all-in on a fad diet just because it helped someone else lose weight. What helped your best friend's kid may not work for yours. You need duplicatable evidence-based strategies with a high universal success rate. All of those personal characteristics are included in the research that backs the science of applied behavior analysis.

These behavioral skills work because the data says so.

As a board-certified behavior analyst, I have collected and utilized these skills across my entire universe. Yes, I teach them, but I also use them with my children, spouse, and family members. In my experience, various behaviors have specific analytical "shades" that guide a person's interactions with other people.

This journey you will embark on won't be based on feeling your way through or allowing your emotions or intuition to call all the shots. To achieve a true breakthrough, you must rely on what the data says will deliver the results that will benefit everyone.

These strategies should become a part of who you are. I believe in these behavioral skills, have seen them work for many people, and have studied the data that proves they work. As a result, I am confident in sharing this knowledge to help you.

The key is daily practice. Rely on proven strategies and persevere!

HOPES LIES AHEAD

Your mental health matters. If you feel tapped out, you are not alone. If your child is in a challenging environment at school, there is hope. If your students have a challenging environment at home, there is hope.

Hope is alive because you woke up this morning and have the opportunity to try again. Holding this book in your hands proves your willingness to learn and change, which is the foundation for gaining instructional control. Life can be challenging and exhausting. The skills in this book allow room for error.

There is no judgment here.

This thing is hard.

And if you aren't hitting roadblocks, that probably means you haven't tried long enough. Roadblocks are inevitable but don't have to lead to dead ends. They also don't mean you should "just keep doing the same thing and hope things will eventually change." I'm here to help you find greater success with proven techniques to lessen your frustration and increase your victories, just like the princesses my daughters love to cheer for and emulate!

There are no heavier burdens than the guilt and shame we often carry. It's time to let it go (easier said than done, but also possible). Being here with me shows your good nature and your willingness to invest in your loved ones or students. Give room for error in being a human. Don't look back at what you have or haven't done as a parent or educator because hope lies ahead.

This book represents a lifestyle change, a way to increase pro-social behavior and decrease challenging behaviors significantly. The strategies are effective, but life happens. New challenges arise, and humans reach the stages of life at different times. *That is why I recommend learning a technique, practicing it, and then coming back and adding another one to your toolbox.*

These behavioral skills work, but the combination and application of each will vary. This book's combination and mastery of each skill provide the ultimate recipe for behavior change. However, the process will lose its efficacy without the ability to learn and implement each in chronological order of priority. Lay the foundation first.

> **Are you being "too strict" or "too gentle?"**
> **You don't even need those parameters or labels**
> **to affect change! So, forget about the gentle**
> **parenting vs. strict parenting debate. It's just noise.**

Don't fall for fads, as tempting as they seem. Fads come and go, but *real* change starts with YOU. Behavior modification isn't accomplished by sending your child to therapy and hoping they return "changed." Lasting change occurs when you modify the environment to impact the behavior in a desired way. It's about learning a new way to interact with those in your care.

As we continue, consider the immense hope you felt when rooting for the hero in your favorite childhood story. Why tap into that? Because that's a feeling that should never fade away, and it's also a feeling that the kids in your life still have.

It may seem like the protagonists (the challenging behaviors) are winning—but hope lies ahead. You can overcome even the most daunting challenges with an open heart and the right strategies (and, in our case, a spoonful of evidence-based behavioral skills).

If you feel like you're barely treading water, I'm here to throw you a lifeline in the form of practical strategies that are proven to make a difference. Together, they will fill your toolkit with instruments like descriptive praise and the first/then approach. We'll also tackle denials head-on, set clear expectations, and use rewards to reinforce prosocial behaviors. Plus, I'll show you how visuals, timers, and even knowing when to hold back on rewards can work like a charm.

Utilizing reinforcement in behavioral therapy is akin to a fairy tale come true. Just as a fairy godmother bestows blessings upon a deserving hero, reinforcement provides the special touch that can transform behaviors and nurture growth.

Before we jump into the first behavioral skill, we'll spend a few more pages introducing you to key concepts and terms that will enable you to get the most out of this book so that it can become your go-to behavioral help field guide!

Mrs. Emerson watched as her teachings took root, and Brightville blossomed into a community where understanding and patience reigned. The journey they had embarked upon together had not only altered behaviors but had also woven a tapestry of empathy and respect. Brightville, once shrouded in frustration, now glowed with the warmth of a community united in its quest for a better tomorrow. And so, under the watchful eyes of the stars, Brightville slept peacefully, a beacon of hope in a world eager for change.

Focusing on reinforcing desired actions and behaviors unlocks a world of possibilities and empowers *anyone* to thrive. As we journey ahead, I encourage you to pay attention to the signposts and apply the transformative tools I give you, resolving to achieve a Behavior Breakthrough.

FOLLOW ME ON FACEBOOK AND JOIN MY PRIVATE GROUP!

Find me on Facebook at **Behavior Breakthrough with Bailey Payne (@baileypaynebcba)**. Like and follow me to see videos, parenting hacks, and plenty of real life as I parent two kiddos as a full-time career mom and wife. We'll laugh at the messy stuff and talk about the good stuff, too!

You can also join our private Facebook group, **Behavior Breakthrough Community**, where you can ask questions and learn from other parents or educators experiencing similar issues. Simply scan the QR code to join!

As Aubrey Daniels says, "Behavior goes where reinforcement flows." That is genius and so true. We should strive to be purposeful in delivering reinforcement with a full understanding of its power over behavior.

CHAPTER 2

Key Terms to Know

A s the townspeople basked in their newfound harmony, Mrs. Emerson gathered the residents of Brightville. She noticed their eagerness to learn and their thirst for deeper understanding. "To truly harness the power of change," she began, her voice echoing with wisdom, "one must first understand the language of transformation."

With a gentle smile, Mrs. Emerson introduced the villagers to the lexicon of ABA—a collection of terms and concepts that were keys to unlocking even greater potential. She spoke of "reinforcement," "instructional control," and more, weaving them into stories that made the complex seem simple.

The parents and educators listened intently, their minds opening to the terminology that would help them better comprehend the strategies they had started to apply. They learned about "antecedents" that set the stage for behavior and "consequences" that shaped its future course.

As Mrs. Emerson explained each term, it was as if she was giving the townspeople a map to navigate the maze of behavior. They began to see their actions and those of their loved ones in a new light, understanding the whys and hows behind each interaction.

For this book to change your life and the lives of those around you, it must be user-friendly and practical. To accomplish that, you need a basic understanding of a few key terms you'll see repeatedly. For me, these words are second nature. But new terms can be intimidating to those who don't come from a behavioral therapy background. So, let's remove that intimidation factor and make it simple.

Note for the most tired and stressed heroes and heroines among us: This chapter is short and sweet, so there's no need to skip it! When implementing new things, it's essential to understand foundational terms. But if you're in a hurry, read the simple definitions of each term before you continue to the next chapter.

UNDESIRED/CHALLENGING BEHAVIOR
Behavior you want to reduce

We'll talk a lot about *challenging* behaviors, which are the *undesired* behaviors you seek to reduce. You make the rules when determining what you consider "undesired" in the home or classroom. You get to decide when a behavior is creating undesired results! You also choose the desired behavior to replace the challenging one with. (A desired behavior is generally the opposite of the undesired one.)

Family dynamics and culture play a huge role in viewing certain behaviors. Every family and classroom has its own culture, so there are no concrete rules on which behaviors are always desired or undesired. For example, in some households, arguing can be undesired behavior. But in your home, that may not be a challenge. You may see arguing as debating or a powerful way to negotiate some need.

Here are some questions to help you determine whether a behavior is undesired:

- **"Does this behavior disrupt life?"** If so, chances are it's an undesired behavior.

- **"Does this behavior happen on a repetitive basis?"** Undesired behaviors happen, and no one is perfect! I give grace, but once it becomes a pattern, it's a problem.

- **"Does this behavior cause me to stop and consistently give corrections or corrective feedback?"** If so, consider it a problem.

- **"Does this behavior create distractions and a loss of productivity?"** If it's disrupting the learning experience in the classroom, it's undesired.

- **"Does this behavior increase frustration?"** If it's disrupting mental health, productivity, and relationships in the home or classroom, it's undesired.

25

DESIRED/PROSOCIAL BEHAVIOR
Behavior you want to reinforce

On the other end of the spectrum are *prosocial* behaviors, which are the more *desired* responses you want to reinforce or encourage. Prosocial behavior refers to voluntary and functional actions intended to benefit others or the learners in the household, classroom, or society. This behavior plays a significant role in understanding a child's development of compassion and moral values.

Some examples of prosocial behaviors are sharing, helping, apologizing, forgiving, cooperating, showing empathy, attending, expressing, and displaying altruism (doing the right thing without expecting a reward).

Encouraging and nurturing prosocial behavior is vital for a person's social and emotional development. You can support the development of prosocial behaviors by modeling prosocial actions, reinforcing desired behavior, fostering empathy and compassion, and providing opportunities for cooperation and shared decision-making. More on those later!

DESIRED OUTCOME
An outcome that achieves the learner's
motivation and, in turn, increases prosocial behavior

The definition of *desired outcomes* is broad, with many applications you can customize to your unique situation. A person's desired outcome is something they enjoy—verbal praise, a tangible (like a toy or treat), or anything else they seek. As you seek a breakthrough, you want to see desired outcomes or prosocial behaviors in others. Desired outcomes will vary from person to person, but these outcomes are essential in increasing prosocial behavior. How?

To achieve the desired outcome, you must promote and encourage functional and prosocial behaviors.

The key here is that what works as a motivator for one child may not be the best solution for another child. It depends on the environment and the person offering the outcome (parent, teacher, etc.). You can determine whether something is a desired outcome by asking, "Does the behavior consistently deliver the results both I and the learner want?" If the answer is yes, that outcome becomes preferred.

REINFORCEMENT
An outcome that leads to more prosocial behavior

Reinforcement is a pretty big deal in this book! When I ask people what they use for reinforcement, I hear answers that range from giving out stickers and high-fives to giving a break and picking from the treasure box. The parents and professionals I work with tend to think of the concept like this:

- When students in the classroom work quietly, the teacher gives them a sticker.
- When a child gets dressed independently, their mother gives them a treat at breakfast.
- When students complete their homework, they earn a piece of candy.
- When a child shares a toy with their sibling, their parents tell them how proud they are.

It's easy to apply this idea and think: "Reward = Reinforcement." However, that's not the fullest or most accurate story—and in fact, this view of reinforcement misses a key element: You can only consider a reward to be *reinforcement* when the desired behavior continues to occur. Here's another way to say it:

Reinforcement leads to an increase in the desired behavior over time.

That is an essential point because not all reinforcements are effective.

According to my definition, if a delivered reinforcement does not result in more desired behavior over time, that's not a reinforcer. If you deliver a reinforcer that does not increase the frequency of desired behavior, stop using it.

Think of it this way: If someone highly introverted raises their hand and answers a question, the teacher may say in front of the class, "Wow, thank you so much for raising your hand. You're right. I can tell you're paying attention. Great work!"

The teacher didn't know it, but that student didn't like the attention. As a result, they no longer raise their hand. That was not a reinforcer. It was a punisher because it decreased the prosocial hand-raising behavior.

So, as we move along, think of reinforcement in terms of whether it increases desired behavior or decreases it. If the desired behavior frequency *decreases*, you've found a punishment, not a reinforcer. In essence, effective reinforcement is all about encouraging more of the behavior we want to see. Always remember, if a strategy leads to less of the desired behavior, then it's acting as a deterrent rather than a motivator.

REINFORCEMENT VS. REWARD
Reinforcement delivers results, while rewards are hit-or-miss.

You should be able to link a behavior increase to a reinforcer directly. If you can't, it's not a reinforcer but a simple reward. A reinforcer should alter behavior by increasing it. For example:

Suppose you have been giving stickers for desired behavior for years but continue to observe the same undesired behaviors; there is no change. In that case, stickers are ineffective reinforcers to increase desired behavior.

Perhaps you let students choose from a prize box if they stop talking and raise their hands. Yet, there are still interruptions. The prize box, then, is not an effective reinforcer if the goal is to encourage quiet, hand-raising behavior.

If you want to increase any behavior, reinforcement has to be present. Remember, reinforcement should increase prosocial behavior. If undesired behaviors persist or increase, then you have probably reinforced the wrong behavior. Therefore, you must deliver reinforcement that targets desired behaviors to increase preferred outcomes.

A reward is something globally referred to as desired or good. But things like stickers, smiley faces on an assignment, candy, high-fives, and ribbons are only rewards, not reinforcements, unless you can tie them *directly back* to increasing the frequency of desired behavior. But in most cases, you can't trace them back because effective reinforcers vary from person to person. Don't get me wrong—rewards are great! Most people enjoy smiley faces or high fives, but these often do not directly increase desired behaviors.

If you are a parent, you can experiment with different reinforcers to see what produces the desired effect (which, of course, is the increased future frequency of desired behavior) in your child. If you are an educator, you can do the same thing with your students—but it needs to be done individually (on a student-by-student basis) rather than applying universal rewards like prize boxes or pizza days. It is possible to establish effective reinforcement for a whole group. Still, you must ensure that each student's behavior increases for the good first, not just a few targeted students. After all, group contingencies should impact the whole group, not just a few.

It's not about what you "think" someone would like. It's about what works to increase the behavior you want to see.

And more than likely, those stickers and that prize box aren't getting the job done because most displays of undesired behaviors are not motivated by accessing smiley faces, high fives, stickers, or treat boxes. The reinforcer lies somewhere else—in data-driven strategies.

DATA-DRIVEN / EVIDENCE-BASED
The foundation of effective behavioral strategies

In behavioral therapy and other sciences, there are two basic types of proof to show that something is effective or ineffective (works or doesn't work): 1) anecdotal proof and 2) evidence-based or data-driven proof.

Anecdotal evidence is like a story or a personal experience that someone tells. It is based on what one person saw or felt, but it might not be true for everyone or even based on data from that reporter's experience.

On the other hand, data-driven evidence comes from collecting information and facts from many different people or sources by observing and counting behaviors. Looking at patterns and trends helps us understand things with factual proof. So, while anecdotes are interesting (your sister-in-law may have good luck with offering money for all As!), data-driven evidence gives us a clearer picture because it looks at information from a bigger group of people or more systematically.

For something to be data-driven, professionals and experts have collected data on behavioral outcomes to ensure its efficacy. It's not based on intuition, hunches, or a few success stories. As parents or educators, we often make decisions based on what we *feel* is best. But if the goal is to change behavior effectively, we must ensure we're making data-driven and evidence-based decisions.

The strategies in this book have been proven through multiple long-term research studies and have shown to be impactful based on data collection procedures across ages, environments, circumstances, developmental functioning levels, diagnoses, and other variables. That's how science tells us that these behavioral skills are data-driven and evidence-based.

Going forward, commit to making solid decisions based not on what you feel but on what science and data say is effective. This book will help you discover tried-and-true strategies to produce the desired behavioral results.

ENVIRONMENT
Stimuli around you that affect behavior

Another term you'll see is *environment.* An environment is every stimulus around a person or group that may impact behavior. Your environment (at home, in the classroom, in the car, at a party, or anywhere else) encompasses everything you see and sense—from the placement of furniture and the people to the lighting and technology. It also includes preferred toys and activities available. The term also encompasses the presence of aversive stimuli, such as loud noises or a crying sibling. Don't forget: if you're in the environment, you and your interactions are part of the environment as well.

Any stimulus can be an environmental variable. By contrast, an environmental contingency is a behavioral response to the environment.

Until you better evaluate the environment and how elements within it motivate behavior, you will not create the impact you need. That's why it's time to evaluate every environment your loved one or learner encounters to change behavior. Why? Because environmental contingencies are what shape behavior.

An *environmental contingency* means that things around us can affect how we behave. It's like when something in our environment makes us take specific actions. For example, if your child receives a desired outcome every time they finish their homework (and you know it's a desired outcome because it makes your kid want to perform that desired behavior more), that desired outcome is an environmental contingency that makes a child want to keep doing their homework.

It's reinforcement that encourages the behavior.

In the same way, if someone has a headache and enters a large department store with bright lights, loud noises, and busy crowds, they may display behaviors to avoid this environment or to leave this environment. They may become less social and stop talking. Maybe they want to go home. They might yell at a department store worker rather than simply asking where the exit is. These are examples of how the environment can influence our behavior (desired or unde-sired) by using environmental variables to impact our behavior.

The environmental contingency in this example may have been when the store clerk pointed at the exit, and the individual left the store to access a quieter environment, finding immediate headache relief. Therefore, yelling at a store clerk was an effective contin-gency for getting their needs met.

Nothing is off limits when referring to the environment. As long as it has a presence, it has an impact in some way.

PREFERENCES
High-value choices

In the most general sense, *preferences* are things a person likes, enjoys, and gravitates towards. If a pile of toys is sitting in front of your child, their preferred toy (or preference) is the one they reach for four out of five times. That selection frequency signals a preference.

Preferences are valuable because they often indicate what may serve as an impactful reinforcer to modify behavior. But a note of caution here: Not every preference is an effective reinforcer. Is there a countable decrease in the incidences of that undesired behavior (that you observed during data collection)? If the answer is no, that preference is not a reinforcer.

In other words, preferences are more about what someone likes, while reinforcers come with data-driven, tangible changes in behavioral displays. Meaningful preferences can tell us what a person values and wants to access strongly enough to engage in less-preferred tasks or activities.

INSTRUCTIONAL CONTROL
A way of managing an environment to
encourage desired behavior and learning

Instructional control refers to utilizing strategies to manipulate an environment to have a desired impact on behavior.

Controlling reinforcement delivery to impact behavior is essential for success in any environment. For example, when a teacher can control how a child learns, it helps create a suitable classroom environment. It also means the teacher can encourage (through reinforcement) the prosocial behaviors they want to see more of, like paying attention and following instructions, while minimizing the undesired behaviors they don't want, like talking out of turn or incorrectly using instructional materials.

When you establish instructional control, you empower everyone to implicitly agree that the environment is a good place for learning or interacting and that no problem hinders a person's success and ability to learn and grow. Instructional control is mastering environmental contingencies and delivering reinforcement to encourage desired behavior.

Armed with knowledge and a new language, the townspeople felt empowered. Their journey of transformation was not just about changing behaviors but also about learning and growing themselves. Brightville's story was unfolding into a tale of enlightenment and empowerment, setting the stage for even more remarkable transformations ahead.

Understanding key terms is fundamental to the effective monitoring of behavioral strategies. These terms serve as the building blocks for collecting valuable data and identifying patterns in behavior. Armed with this knowledge, you can move to the next chapter, where we'll explore the significance of monitoring efficacy to ensure that your chosen behavioral interventions positively impact the lives of those you care for.

Trust your gut!

But back it up with data!

CHAPTER 3

Monitor Efficacy to Track Progress

With the people of Brightville becoming more fluent in the language of transformation, Mrs. Emerson saw it was time to introduce them to the tools of mastery—the ways to monitor efficacy and track progress. She gathered the community under the grand oak in the village square, her eyes twinkling with knowledge and purpose.

"Dear friends," she began, "to ensure our journey towards growth is on the right path, we must learn to measure our progress." She introduced them first to "Frequency Data," likening it to counting the stars in the night sky. "Just as each star brightens the heavens, each instance of a behavior, desired or otherwise, illuminates our understanding," she explained. She taught them how to count and record these instances, turning observations into valuable insights.

Next, Mrs. Emerson unveiled the concept of "ABC Notes," a method as simple yet profound as a storyteller's narrative. "A stands for Antecedent, B for Behavior, and C for Consequence," she said. The townspeople learned to observe what happened before and after a behavior, like piecing together a story, to understand and shape the chapters of their lives.

Finally, she introduced them to "Momentary Time Sampling," a method as intriguing as it sounded. "This is like capturing a snapshot at regular intervals," she elucidated. "It helps us see the bigger picture, to understand how often a behavior occurs without needing constant vigilance."

Armed with these three powerful tools, the townspeople felt a renewed sense of control and direction. They began to apply these techniques, tracking and observing, turning their daily experiences into data to guide them further.

Imagine if you possessed a secret lens capable of unveiling the inner workings of the behavioral skills you will discover in this book, allowing you to navigate the path to success, peace, and joy with precision and confidence and, most importantly, proof that you're walking the right path.

Such a lens exists, and its name is efficacy monitoring.

Like a compass guiding you through uncharted waters, efficacy monitoring is a most valued companion as you learn and incorporate behavioral strategies in your home, classroom, or community. It's a tool that allows you to measure, assess, and adjust your interventions, ensuring they hit the bullseye of maximum impact. It also allows you to avoid investing in strategies that aren't achieving desired results. After all, we're all already stretched thin, so let's maximize our efforts.

But what exactly is efficacy monitoring, and why is it so crucial? Picture it as a powerful magnifying glass, allowing you to zoom in on the details of your interventions. It goes beyond observation, clearly understanding how a strategy is (or is not) influencing a child's behavior.

EFFICACY MONITORING

The systematic and ongoing process of observing and measuring the effectiveness of behavior interventions or strategies. It involves tracking and evaluating behavioral trends to determine whether the techniques achieve the desired outcomes or need modifications to support a child's growth and development.

Efficacy monitoring is not passive; it requires active engagement and dedication. So, in this chapter, we will discuss the tools and techniques that empower you to assess the effectiveness of your interventions, shedding light on the wins and challenges you may encounter along the way. This process is a critical step in refining your approach and ensuring that your strategies are truly making a positive impact.

THE IMPORTANCE OF BASELINES AND GOALS

For something to be evidence-based, you need—wait for it—evidence. Another way to say it is that you need collected data that becomes evidence of a strategy's effectiveness. There must be tangible proof that your actions are working to produce the outcomes you want.

If you're reading this, I know you're ready to pour your heart and soul into changing your interactions with others to decrease challenging behaviors and increase desired ones. So, that also means you want to be sure your actions are effective. After all, when you are present, you are a part of the environment and provide environmental contingencies.

What you need to ensure success is *baseline data* for comparison.

Having a baseline number when collecting data is crucial because it gives you a starting point to measure progress. A baseline number shows how things are before you utilize a new behavioral skill. It's like a "before" picture when you're on a health journey. Without a baseline, you wouldn't know if a strategy is making a difference because you wouldn't have anything to compare it to.

Using a behavioral strategy without collecting baseline data is like starting lifestyle habit changes without knowing your body measurements or weight beforehand. We are all motivated by changing numbers in the desired direction.

Initially, you may want to lose weight so your clothes fit properly, but it takes motivation and work to keep the pounds off. In the end, what counts is the number of inches or pounds you've lost.

Baselines help you see the changes over time and understand if the new strategy moves behavior frequencies in the right direction (i.e., less frequent for the challenging ones, more frequent for the prosocial ones). That number becomes a valuable tool that helps track progress and ensure the behavioral strategy is helping achieve goals and improve behavior.

Your data collection can be basic—whether you mark on a calendar, use the notes section in your smartphone, keep a few sticky notes with you, email yourself, or buy a cute notebook expressly for this purpose, make it natural to start recording data on things like:

- Common problem behaviors
- Challenging behavior frequency
- Common problems from teacher reports

It's also helpful to monitor your frustration level. Choose a scale (1 to 5 works well) and record your daily frustration level. Set parameters that work for your situation and your life. Here is one suggestion.

FRUSTRATION LEVEL PARAMETERS

1. **LEVEL 1:** Highest levels of compliance, desired behaviors, and peace

2. **LEVEL 2:** A few sporadic challenging behaviors but an overall joyful day

3. **LEVEL 3:** Increased levels of frustration and environmental disruptions

4. **LEVEL 4:** Heightened challenging behaviors that tested patience and caused significant disruptions

5. **LEVEL 5:** Drained of patience and joy and utterly spent from a day full of challenging behavior

> **NOTE:** This scale is subjective in nature. But since you are not submitting your findings for peer review, you can use whatever scale tracks and monitors your biggest concerns. If tracking your frustration levels along with your strategy data results helps you assess progress, then go for it!

Why is tracking so important? If you're pouring your heart into changing your language and interactions with others, you should know whether it's impacting the behavior in your home or other environments.

Otherwise, what's the point?

Are challenging behaviors decreasing? Do you see new desired skills emerge, such as asking for snacks appropriately and raising their hands more?

If you continue to do the same thing every day but expect different results, that is self-inflicted pain—and it's also the definition of insanity. You need goals so that you know what you're trying to achieve! Here is a list of simple goals you can set at the beginning of this process as you learn these behavioral strategies:

1. **Increase Positive Reinforcement:** Aim to provide more frequent and specific praise or rewards to reinforce desired behaviors.

2. **Improve Compliance:** Work towards increasing willingness to follow instructions and rules with a certain number of reminders.

3. **Reduce Challenging Behaviors:** Set a goal to decrease the occurrence of specific challenging behaviors through appropriate interventions (this can be activity-based or time-based).

4. **Enhance Communication:** Focus on improving communication skills, such as using words to express needs and emotions or appropriately requesting a break before problematic behaviors emerge.

5. **Develop Social Skills:** Encourage prosocial interactions, such as sharing, taking turns, and showing empathy.

6. **Improve Self-Regulation:** Help develop the ability to manage emotions and control impulses by identifying emotions and using problem-solving skills before problematic behaviors occur.

7. **Increase Task Completion:** Work towards improving completing tasks and assignments independently or without the display of challenging behavior.

8. **Foster Independence:** Set a goal to promote self-help skills, allowing space and opportunities to perform tasks independently (without assistance, reminders, or attentional interactions).

9. **Enhance Focus and Attention:** Aim to increase focus and attention during tasks or activities by decreasing off-task comments and leaving the instructional area during activities or increasing accuracy in answering comprehension questions after reading a passage.

10. **Reduce Anxiety or Avoidance:** Work towards helping to cope with anxiety and avoidant behaviors in challenging situations (decrease verbal refusals of "no," decrease laying head down during tasks, or increase overall reported comfort levels).

This is an amazing list, right? Who wouldn't want to achieve these things in their lives? I'm telling you it's possible when you achieve Behavior Breakthrough.

If you go through the effort, you might as well make the action effective. That means you need goals. Setting clear, achievable, and *specific* goals when using a new behavioral strategy will provide direction and help track progress. Remember to set specific goals. Avoid vague goals, such as "Be nicer" and "Work harder." (What do you mean by "nicer"? How will you determine if the child is working "harder"?)

You are in the driver's seat when deciding how to collect evidence on behavioral changes. For example, collecting data on "decreasing anger" would be challenging, but collecting data on decreasing "yelling in an angry tone paired with task refusal" is more specific and easier to track progress.

Now it's your turn. Write down THREE GOALS you wish to accomplish by reading this book and implementing its strategies. (Be specific!):

1.

2.

3.

Be patient and consistently implement the chosen techniques while celebrating small successes. By progressing towards these goals, you and your loved ones will create a supportive environment and foster growth.

I regularly consult with parents and professionals who want to know how to invest their time using therapeutic interventions. They want me to pick the most meaningful goals and therapies for their loved ones based on the skill deficits or the challenges they present. Here is how that conversation usually sounds (and my answer is always the same):

Them: "Can you just tell me what to do to stop this behavior? I can't take it anymore! Tell me what therapies we need and what to do!"

Me: "I don't know the exact recipe that will positively impact your loved one. However, we can collect data on targeted behaviors you wish to alter and determine what strategies and therapies have a desired impact. Then, you can invest in what matters to your loved one. Recommendations based on guesses, assumptions, or emotions will have a significantly lower impact because they're not data-driven."

There is merit to those gut feelings you have. However, don't stop at that intuitive or gut instinct. The next step is to collect data to prove that your gut feeling is justified. So, pick three target areas and start recording today! Consider these questions:

- Do you want to start recording the frequency of tantrums surrounding mealtime?
- What about a refusal to bathe or brush their teeth?

- Do you want to decrease your teen's refusal to limit social media time?
- Are you looking to decrease talking during class assignments?

Choose the behaviors you wish to target and start tracking them now! This data collection—which occurs before you attempt a strategy—is the baseline. The baseline provides a critical "comparison number," which can help you assess whether a strategy is working.

PRO TIP FOR NOVICE DATA COLLECTORS:
TARGET ONE BEHAVIOR CONSISTENTLY ACROSS TIME

If you collect data on tantrums one day, aggression the next day, and functional communication the next, that data will not provide valuable comparison baselines.

Choose an area or multiple areas. (I recommend targeting one behavior at a time so that the data is helpful). But whatever or however much you choose to track, do so daily. That's how you successfully monitor efficacy. If you forget to collect data (because life gets busy) and record in a "data dump" fashion at the end of the week, your data will be skewed by feelings, emotions, and memory. As a result, you won't have a clear picture of intervention effectiveness. So, set a timer on your phone or set a routine to document your data at the same time every day.

Based on your goals and the outcomes you wish to achieve, collect data on those goals and ensure that your daily data collection corresponds with the objectives. Even if the number is zero, it is vital to record.

THREE DATA-
COLLECTION METHODS

This process can feel daunting when you are a parent of multiple children, a teacher dealing with an entire classroom that may need intervention, the caregiver for someone with elevated needs, or a single or working parent. I want to break down three realistic data-collection methods so you can choose the method or methods that best fit your unique situation. The investment in data collection will serve you well in the long run. It will keep you from wasting time on ineffective methods and making emotion-based decisions. Instead, you can focus on behavioral skills that actually work!

These data-collection strategies are not so precise that you'd see them in a research study setting, but they are perfect for real life. Rather than depending on anecdotes and gut feelings, you can rely on realistic, applicable ways to make data-driven assessments.

Method #1: Frequency Data

FREQUENCY DATA
Record the number of times a
behavior occurs in a set period.

The first data-collection strategy is frequency. The frequency of a behavior is the number of times it occurs in a set period (e.g., during math class, the morning routine, or recess). It's far less daunting to track a smaller period than broadly set it as "all the time."

Broad behavioral labels (aggression, tantrums, defiance, etc.) could include other behaviors and skew your data. So, be specific when identifying the behavior you want to track. For example, you could track:

- **Hitting others during recess**
- **Inconsolable crying that lasts longer than five minutes**
- **Talking while the teacher is talking**

These descriptions all detail more specific behaviors and will result in accurate data, allowing you to determine whether your interventions are changing particular behaviors.

CLASSROOM EXAMPLE

Let's say you are a teacher tracking a student's tendency to "touch peers during circle time." To collect frequency data, you will mark tallies on a sticky note or whiteboard each time you see the student you are monitoring physically contact another student during circle time.

Once you have that data and see a pattern over multiple days, implement a strategy (one you will learn about the strategies later in this book). Address the behavior and continue tracking the same data (mark the same tallies and monitor the same behavior) for the same period. You will begin to see whether that strategy is effective.

Did the frequency of touching peers during circle time decrease contingent upon your strategy implementation? It's a simple yes or no—and now you have proof to justify your decisions as an educator! If the strategy doesn't seem to be working, ask yourself a few key questions:

- **Did I miss a step during implementation?**
- **Am I reinforcing the desired behavior?**
- **Am I inadvertently doing or saying something that is reinforcing wrong behavior?**
- **How can I adjust the process to become more effective?**

HOME EXAMPLE

It works the same at home. Let's say you want to track hitting behavior toward siblings during the morning routine before school. First, you need your baseline. So, grab a sticky note or your phone and track every occurrence of hitting behavior during a set time frame.

Baseline achieved! Then, execute the strategy and continue to track.

Did the incidences of hitting siblings begin to decrease when you implemented a strategy? This simple frequency data gives you all the necessary information to make sound decisions to guide your child to display prosocial behavior.

You can take it a step further and transfer those tally marks to a daily calendar with a few quick notes so you can compare and continue monitoring efficacy. That will give you trends across days to examine the bigger picture.

For some behaviors, collecting frequency data is more challenging. That is the case for behaviors with an extremely high rate of frequency (i.e., it happens so often that you're not sure there are enough sticky notes to handle all the tally marks!). If it is too difficult to determine the start and end of a behavior, frequency data may not be the best option. Frequency data may not be the best fit for high-occurring behaviors or behaviors simultaneously occurring with multiple other undesired behaviors.

In other words, frequency data is only useful if the behavior happens at a rate you can count easily.

The purpose of investing time and energy into collecting frequency data is to determine how often the behavior occurs. That way, you have a baseline to tell if the frequency decreases. Here are the steps to record and utilize frequency data:

FREQUENCY DATA COLLECTION SUMMARY

1. Pick a set period to track a defined behavior. Choose a short duration (not "all day") unless the behavior rarely occurs.
2. Keep a sticky note handy. A notebook and phone notes app work, too.
3. Record each incidence of that behavior during the period. That is your baseline.
4. Implement a strategy and continue to record incidences of that behavior during the period.
5. Compare new tally marks to your baseline.
6. Note whether there is improvement. If so, continue implementing the strategy. If not, adjust.

Note: Even after implementing the strategy, it may take several days to determine if the behavior has changed. Keep tracking the behavior. Eventually, you should be able to tell whether the behavior has increased, decreased, or remained the same.

Without collecting several days or weeks of data, you may prematurely determine strategy effectiveness with no real evidence to support your conclusion.

Method #2: ABC Notes

ABC NOTES

Record the environmental trigger, the behavioral response to the trigger, and the consequences of that behavior.

The next data-collection method is called *"three-term contingency data collection."* It involves collecting data on three essential components of a behavioral event: antecedents, behaviors, and consequences. But that's a mouthful, so we'll call it an *ABC note*, with the letters standing for three things you will record:

Antecedents (Triggers): These are events or triggers that occur before a behavior happens. They can be environmental factors, instructions given, private thoughts or feelings a person has, or specific situations that influence behavior.

Behaviors (Responses): This refers to the observable actions or responses displayed in response to the antecedents. It involves recording the specific behavior, such as talking out of turn, failing to raise their hand, and talking excessively about a single topic.

Consequences (Outcomes): These are the outcomes or results that follow the behavior. Positive consequences should lead to an increase in the desired behavior. By contrast, negative consequences should result in a decrease in undesired behavior. Either way, consequences hold the power to change behavior.

To conduct a three-term contingency collection (ABC note), record each component of the behavioral event when it occurs. This information will become invaluable for you! It helps you analyze patterns and relationships between *antecedents* (triggers), *behaviors* (responses), and *consequences* (outcomes). It also allows you to understand the patterns for certain behaviors and develop effective interventions to modify or reinforce them. Understanding the data regarding a pattern of consistent contingencies also enables you to start making behavioral predictions.

Consider a practical example of ABC recording in a classroom:

- **Antecedent:** The teacher announces it's time for group reading activities. She expects the class to sit quietly and begin reading.
- **Behavior:** During the reading activity, Sarah starts to tap her pencil loudly on the desk and makes distracting noises.
- Consequence: **The teacher approaches Sarah and asks** her to stop tapping the pencil. The teacher must also redirect the class's attention to the reading activity.

The teacher may record a shorter version in her ABC Notes:

- **Antecedent:** I announce the group reading activity.
- **Behavior:** Sarah begins tapping her pencil and making disruptive noises.
- **Consequence:** I must stop and address the behavior and redirect everyone's attention.

By recording this ABC data during multiple instances of the behavior, Sarah's teacher can identify patterns and potential triggers that lead to Sarah's pencil tapping. The teacher should be as detailed as possible! Does the behavior occur just during reading time? Does it happen when Sarah reads in small groups? Does the tapping occur whenever I make a classroom request?

The teacher can also identify patterns of outcomes that may be maintaining Sarah's pencil-tapping behavior. Does she consistently receive reprimands and redirections from the teacher across a pattern of data collection days? If so, this could indicate that Sarah's pencil-tapping behavior is maintained and potentially reinforced by attention from the teacher. This information can guide Sarah's teacher in choosing targeted interventions. Once the teacher introduces a strategy, she should continue to take ABC notes surrounding Sarah's behavior.

This collection method can be more time-consuming but produces tremendously useful data. It has become a highly natural form of data collection for many clients. Why? Because it's common for us to reflect on things in hindsight, spot what triggered the behavior, and evaluate the outcome.

With consistent tracking, you can find the pattern of consistent antecedents, behaviors, and consequences. You understand why the behavior is happening and can select more effective strategies.

Briefly summarize the incident from start to finish as you mentally replay it. It doesn't take a lot of practice to reflect on a situation and write it down. But it does take practice to start counting behaviors in the form of tally marks. So, each method has its benefits and hurdles to overcome. Here are the steps to record and utilize ABC notes:

ABC NOTETAKING SUMMARY

1. Identify a specific behavior you seek to address.

2. Briefly record each portion of a behavioral event after it occurs: Note the antecedent (trigger), the behavior (response), and the consequences (outcome).

3. Analyze the triggers that led to the behavior and the outcomes (what changed in the environment after the behavior). That is your baseline.

4. Implement a behavioral skill and continue to record the ABCs surrounding that behavior.

5. Compare new ABC notes to your baseline ABC notes. Are behaviors happening just as much? Have you documented just as many notes? Are the behaviors changing?

6. Note whether there is improvement and continue or make adjustments.

——————— ANTECEDENT EXERCISE ———————

An antecedent is an event or situation that occurs immediately before a particular behavior occurs. It is the trigger or stimulus that sets the stage for the behavior to happen. Understanding antecedents is helpful because they can influence and predict how someone will respond or behave in a given situation.

Write down one undesired behavior you desire to change.

For the next few days, pay special attention to what happens JUST before the behavior occurs (the antecedent). Can you affect or limit that stimulus in some way? If so, how?

By understanding antecedents, you can identify patterns and triggers, allowing you to develop strategies to modify undesired behaviors before they happen.

Method #3: Momentary Time Sampling

——————— MOMENTARY TIME SAMPLING ———————

Collect data only at predetermined intervals.

The final data-collection method is "momentary time sampling." This method utilizes an interval data collection (unlike frequency tallies or after-the-fact ABC notetaking).

With momentary time sampling (sometimes called "interval data collection"), you break up the day into segments. And when that segment ends, document whether the behavior in question is happening at that precise moment.

This type of collection is helpful for extremely busy people who don't have the bandwidth to keep tally marks or record anecdotal ABC notes.

NOTE: This data-collection method is only beneficial for high-frequency behaviors (ones that happen often). You will be sampling the environment in time chunks, so if a sample doesn't record any data about the behaviors, but you know they are occurring, then this data-collection method isn't practical for that specific behavior.

You may be dealing with persistent interruptions or blurting out in the classroom. Or your child will not sit still due to sensory feedback behavior. Here's how it works:

Set a timer to go off every five minutes (or at an interval you choose) for a set number of intervals. At the end of each interval, record whether your child or student is actively engaging in the behavior. If collecting data all day, the time intervals may be hourly. If collecting during a set period (as in dinnertime), the time chunks may be more like five minutes.

It's like taking a snapshot of the moment.

If the behavior is happening when the timer alerts you, record a plus (+). If you do not see the behavior, record a minus (-). Then reset your timer (a silent smartwatch timer that vibrates on your wrist is perfect for this). When it alerts you again, that's your prompt to look for and record the presence (+) or absence (-) of that behavior.

Let's say you are tracking "exiting seat" behavior (leaving one's desk without permission) in the classroom. You follow the behavior over five 5-minute intervals during a class discussion. Suppose you notice the undesired behavior when the timer notifies you at two of five intervals. In that case, it becomes documentation that "leaving one's seat" behavior occurred in 40 percent (2 divided by 5) of the momentary time samples. You can conclude:

"As determined from a sampling of data collection intervals, this student displays exiting seat behavior approximately 40 percent of the time during group discussions."

That gives you valuable data to monitor change over time. After implementing an intervention strategy, is that 40 percent baseline improving, worsening, or staying the same?

Be cautious that your data collection results do not overrepresent or underrepresent what is happening in "real life." This data-collection method works best for behaviors that occur often but are not so frequent that a time sample would underrepresent how often the behavior is actually happening. Let's say a behavior typically happens a few times an hour. In that case, you may pick fifteen-minute intervals and attempt to capture that momentary time sample to represent the frequency of that behavior in the environment.

Time sampling is also best for behaviors lasting at least a few countable seconds or more. For example, catching a sampling of yelling "no!" when the timer sounds would be challenging. But catching sleeping or head-down behavior would be easier since those behaviors typically last longer.

> **NOTE:** You misrepresent reality if you don't capture most occurrences of the behavior from a sampling. Also, if you monitor rarely-occurring behaviors and capture them often during sampling, they may appear to occur in more significant percentages than in reality.

Once you have your baseline, you can implement a strategy to address the behavior and continue to utilize time sampling. Comparing the before and after samples will tell you whether the energy you invest in impacting behavior is worth it. Here are the steps to record and utilize momentary time sampling:

MOMENTARY TIME SAMPLING SUMMARY

1. Define a behavior you wish to track over a set period, then break up the period into defined segments. (e.g., divide one hour into four periods of fifteen minutes each, or divide half an hour into six segments of five minutes each.)

2. Set a timer to alert you at your chosen intervals. A phone or smartwatch works well for this.

3. When the timer sounds, record whether the behavior

is present (+) or absent (-) at that moment. You only need to notice if the behavior occurs when the timer signals you, not total occurrences over the past interval. These results will provide the baseline data.

4. Implement a behavioral skill and record the presence or absence of that behavior at the end of each interval.

5. Compare new momentary time samplings (snapshots of that behavior) to your baseline sampling.

6. Note whether there is improvement and continue or make adjustments.

DATA IS THE WAY

Let's wrap up this discussion as you establish more significant goals. What are you hoping to accomplish by reading this book?

Do you want your child to display more functional communication where they can express their needs and desires appropriately before tantrum behavior starts?

Is there a student who is significantly disrupting the environment? What is one behavior they display that makes the most profoundly negative impact? How would you like to see that behavior change?

Whatever the goal is, make sure that your data collection matches.

Parents and professionals often tell me, "I don't know about continuing with this speech therapy [insert other therapies or interventions]. I'm just not sure we're seeing any progress."

You can't expect to see any progress if you aren't tracking it. So get tracking!

COLLECTION PRO TIP:
STAY FAITHFUL TO YOUR CHOSEN
DATA-COLLECTION METHOD

Find a data-collection method that fits you, your environment, and the behaviors you wish to track, then stick with it. You can only compare three-term contingency data (ABC notes) to other ABC notes. You can only compare frequency tally marks to tally marks. You can only compare momentary time-sampling data to time-sampling data. You can't switch back and forth between collection methods and have anything meaningful to compare.

Start collecting data on your child's or students' behaviors. Once you have those baselines, you can continue tracking as you utilize therapy or these new skills. Then, you have valuable data on what directly impacts the environment and corresponding behaviors.

The people of Brightville had not only the strategies and the language but also the means to measure their progress, ensuring their journey toward a harmonious life was guided by wisdom and insight.

We've covered the basics of monitoring efficacy, so we're ready to learn techniques for making kindness, helpfulness, and sharing happen A LOT more often. With these ideas, you'll have the power to experience a breakthrough as you spread joy, empathy, and compassion wherever you go.

BONUS DATA-COLLECTION TEMPLATES

Here are some data-collection templates you can use to start tracking behaviors using one of the three tracking methods presented in this chapter. Make sure you get your baselines! They are the key to noting the effectiveness or ineffectiveness of the strategies you are about to learn.

FREQUENCY DATA COLLECTION

DATE	BEHAVIOR 1	BEHAVIOR 2	BEHAVIOR 3

ABC DATA COLLECTION

DATE/TIME	ANTECEDENT	BEHAVIOR	CONSEQUENCE

MOMENTARY TIME SAMPLING DATA COLLECTION

BEHAVIOR 1:_____

ACTIVITY:_____

INTERVAL LENGTH:_____

DATE	INTERVAL 1	INTERVAL 2	INTERVAL 3	INTERVAL 4	INTERVAL 5

To download these and other templates,
visit **BaileyPayne.com/Breakthrough** to get
your digital copies now for free!

PART II

THE TWELVE KEYS TO TRANSFORMATION

There is no magic formula that will instantly fix problematic behaviors. However, there DOES exist a group of skills that, when employed correctly and in tandem with tracking data, can create transformational results.

Still, it's important to reiterate that this book isn't something you casually flip through as you search for a quick fix. You don't read one strategy, give it a shot, and expect miraculous behavior changes.

Instead, focus on building a solid foundation, one layer at a time—and in the order they are presented in this book. As you master each behavioral skill, you'll be more equipped to respond to new behaviors as they arise.

Even better, you'll be able to PREVENT problematic behaviors before they occur! Because really, that's the goal—to create a world where everyone focuses on *prevention* rather than reaction.

In a world focused on prevention, you'd feel empowered to proactively increase prosocial behaviors in thriving environments rather than struggle to address problematic behaviors in stressful ones.

You can do this! The breakthrough you need is ahead!

Most people want to please others. They want to know what they are doing well. Receiving detailed feedback, then, is a powerful motivator, prompting people to do their best.

BEHAVIORAL SKILL 1

Descriptive Praise

In the peaceful town of Brightville, there lived a boy named Ethan Thompson. One afternoon, his parents received a call from Ethan's school. The teacher told them that Ethan was having difficulty following instructions and managing his emotions. Concerned about their son's behavior, Mr. and Mrs. Thompson sought help from the town expert, Mrs. Emerson.

Mrs. Emerson believed in the power of reinforcement and introduced a technique called "descriptive praise." She encouraged the parents to acknowledge and praise Ethan's specific behaviors so that he gained confidence. She told them to recognize the good choices he is already making and encourage him to demonstrate more favorable behaviors.

Mrs. Emerson explained how descriptive praise works. Instead of using general statements like, "Good job," she asked them to be specific. Mrs. Emerson wanted them to describe the particular behaviors they wished to see and pair their comments with praise. The goal was to help Ethan understand what he was doing well, enabling him to repeat those actions in the future. She said constructive, specific feedback would motivate their son to make better choices. Descriptive praise for desired behaviors would have a greater impact than corrective feedback for disruptive behaviors.

The next day, Ethan's parents put descriptive praise into action. As his mother called him into dinner, Ethan began picking up his Legos without being asked (something they had asked him to do repeatedly in the past). She smiled and said, "Ethan, I noticed how responsible you are. You took the initiative to clean up your Legos without me even mentioning it. That's amazing!"

Ethan's eyes lit up as he received this personalized praise. He felt a sense of accomplishment and wanted to receive more praise like that in the future. A few weeks passed, and Ethan's parents noticed gradual changes in his behavior. He showed improvement in listening, following instructions, and controlling his emotions. Ethan's self-esteem soared as he received daily descriptive praise for his efforts and achievements. Consequently, Ethan's parents felt more hopeful and fueled by positivity as they made a targeted effort to notice the good in Ethan.

One day, Ethan was completing his morning routine before school and got himself dressed without reminders or getting distracted. Ethan's dad stopped by his room and said, "Ethan, I'm so proud of you this morning! You're getting dressed quickly and all by yourself! I haven't had to remind you once, and I'm so thankful for your hard work this morning! It really helps me out!"

Ethan felt good about himself, knowing his actions

were recognized and appreciated. Driven by descriptive praise, Ethan continued to develop his prosocial behaviors, becoming a role model for his sister and the other children in his Brightville Elementary classroom.

Ethan's parents discovered a simple but powerful tool that helped change how their son acted. Descriptive praise is one of my favorite behavioral skills because it requires so little from parents and educators but delivers massive results! It's about noticing the good and changing how you speak to loved ones and students. More importantly, it's also about acknowledging the good in challenging moments.

Descriptive praise can shift the focus from seeking attention through disruptive acts to embracing cooperation and kindness as a means to positive reinforcement. This chapter will delve into the nuances of this strategy, offering practical tips on integrating descriptive praise into daily interactions.

As we discuss descriptive praise, the goal is to change your language in a way that increases the frequency of desired behavior. Targeted praise can transform the way you interact with others. By focusing on specific, positive feedback, you create an environment where motivation and self-esteem flourish, fostering more of the behaviors you wish to encourage.

ESSENTIALS
The Basics of Descriptive Praise

When you offer descriptive praise, you highlight things you want to see more of, primarily actions and attitudes you are grateful for (prosocial or desired behaviors).

DESCRIPTIVE PRAISE

A form of praise for desired behavior; it describes the specific actions, words, or attitudes you want to reinforce.

"Nice job" and "You're amazing" are generic statements that do not describe the desired behavior you want to see more in the future. General praise or "way to go" statements let a person know you like something they did or said. However, they don't help increase the future frequency of desired behaviors because they are too generic. You could be praising any behavior or another element in the environment.

Descriptive praise is not generic. With descriptive praise, there should be no doubt that certain attitudes, actions, or words make you grateful. Here are some examples of descriptive praise:

- "I love how you walked into the kitchen, picked up your dirty plate, and put it into the sink."
- "Thank you so much for raising your hand and keeping a quiet voice until I called your name before speaking."
- "I love how you walked past your favorite snacks with your hands down and then sat and waited your turn."

Notice there are no negative words. There are no "you didn't" statements. Descriptive praise does not highlight something the child DIDN'T do. It's all about what they did. Descriptive praise acknowledges desired behaviors and shows gratitude while minimizing attention to undesired behaviors. Avoid labeling the undesired behaviors or giving them your attention, and instead focus on the good!

REASONING
Why Descriptive Praise Works

Why is it important to describe the precise behaviors you want to see? There has been a mountain of research on this topic, and here are a few reasons why descriptive praise is so effective:

1. Descriptive praise is more meaningful than vague compliments.

Imagine staying late at work to complete a big project, going above and beyond to complete the task. Which of these two responses would be more meaningful to you: 1) Your boss walks by and mutters, "Hey, good job!" or 2) Your boss stops and says, "I see you're staying late, and I want to acknowledge the extra effort. Your diligence is impressive, and I'm grateful for you and your hard work!"

Every one of us would prefer the second response. We want encouraging feedback that doesn't feel generic. We want to improve our performance. More importantly, we want to hear from people we respect. Descriptive praise carries with it genuine gratitude for our efforts. As a result, we are much more likely to exceed our previous efforts.

2. Descriptive praise boosts language comprehension.

Descriptive praise enhances language capabilities and under-standing, thus increasing the contingency of more desired responses. Here's what that means: For learners struggling with language (more on that in a minute), descriptive praise provides them with words that pair with their desired behaviors, helping them connect descriptions and actions. Put another way:

When you catch your child doing something right and use descriptive words to explain what they did, those words provide a clear pathway to more frequent desired behaviors in the future.

Why is this so critical? Let's say your child has some expressive or receptive language deficits. Descriptive praise connects words with feelings. Here is how I describe the language deficits:

- **Expressive language deficits (issues with expressing):** Expressive language is how we *express* our thoughts and feelings. It includes making requests, labeling, or commenting. People with this type of deficit find it hard to put their thoughts into words, signs, or gestures. They may be unable to find the right words to say what they want. Overall, they struggle to talk or write in a way others can understand.

- **Receptive language deficits (issues with understanding):** Receptive language is about *understanding* what others say, write, or indicate. That can include deficits in following directions, listening to a speaker, and comprehending the message. It's like when someone tells you something, and you have difficulty figuring out what they mean.

When someone has trouble with either expressive or receptive language, it can challenge communication and understanding. Descriptive praise helps people with language deficits in these ways:

1. **It provides clear feedback:** Descriptive praise tells a person precisely what they did well, like using words to ask for help or following instructions. It can also consistently pair behaviors with labels to increase comprehension.

2. **It boosts confidence:** Descriptive praise helps discriminate between desired and undesired attention by repeatedly pairing praise with desired behaviors.

3. **It helps people learn by example:** When adults use descriptive praise, it shows children how to express themselves better.

4. **It motivates people to keep going:** Descriptive praise for their effort and progress encourages loves ones to practice desired behavior while overcoming challenges.

5. **It creates a stronger bond:** Descriptive praise creates an uplifting environment that helps children trust and connect with adults.

Here is another example showing how descriptive praise provides loved ones and learners with the language they need to increase desired behaviors. Let's say you're trying to promote "nice hands" behavior in response to episodes where children were hitting or shoving someone. The following insert explains "nice hands" behavior. In this case, descriptive praise gives children the language they need to protect their boundaries and personal space while addressing problematic behavior.

WHAT ARE "NICE HANDS?"

Behavioral therapists refer to "nice hands" to encourage appropriate behavior related to hands and physical contact. It is a way of acknowledging and reinforcing desired behaviors connected to hand usage. It may sound funny, but remember, we don't want to label or give attention to the undesired behavior.

When a parent, educator, or therapist says "nice hands," they are talking about actions, such as using soft touches, keeping hands to oneself, using hands for appropriate activities, reaching for or relinquishing items gently, or following specific instructions related to hand movements.

For example, if a child typically grabs objects aggressively, you might say "nice hands" as a part of your descriptive praise when the child picks up an object gently and without force. That reinforces the desired behavior and helps the child understand what they did well so they can repeat the desired behavior.

The phrase serves as a simple reminder for children to use their hands appropriately and respectfully, promoting self-control, safety, and appropriate social interactions.

NOTE: You can generalize the "nice hands" concept to all ages and cognitive functioning levels by labeling it "respecting space" or "body control."

What are you teaching when you repeatedly say "nice hands"? Without commanding, you let children know they are demonstrating the desired action; in other words, they are using their hands appropriately. Over time, children are more likely to have their "nice hands" down at their sides instead of pinching or hitting someone because you consistently paired their prosocial behavior with descriptive praise.

This type of praise teaches young ones the language they need. It also increases the contingency that the child will display the desired behavior in the future.

If you want to reinforce "nice hands" in the classroom or at home, catch a child displaying the action you want to see and point it out *immediately* when you notice the behavior. Although descriptive praise can still be effective if there is a delay, you should provide prompt feedback for maximum impact. Offering immediate descriptive praise is especially important for people with language or cognitive deficits or those with severe behavioral challenges.

3. Descriptive praise motivates (but be aware of timing in group settings).

Most people are motivated to please or do well, and descriptive praise utilizes that fact. Human nature drives us to seek approval. This inherent motivation forms the cornerstone of descriptive praise. Delivering specific, descriptive feedback on someone's actions or behavior validates their efforts and amplifies their desire to succeed and please.

That's why descriptive praise is more than just acknowledging something good; it acts as a catalyst, enhancing the frequency and intensity of a person's motivation to perform well. By focusing on the "what" and "how" of their actions, descriptive praise makes the recognition more personal and impactful, leading to a lasting increase in motivation and a sense of satisfaction.

However, not everyone likes public attention in a group setting. So, keep that in mind as you deliver descriptive praise. If you know a student is shy or prefers not to be called out, offer their descriptive praise one-on-one. That may mean it can't happen the moment they display the behavior, but that's okay. It will still have a positive effect by spelling out exactly what they did to increase peace, joy, and cooperation. You can give them specific feedback discretely or one-on-one.

APPLICATION
Descriptive Praise in Action

Now, let's break down some descriptive praise statements across three environments: home, classroom, and community. You'll see how easy it is to use this behavioral skill right away.

DESCRIPTIVE PRAISE IN THE HOME

Reinforcing routines at home is an excellent way to use descriptive praise. Family members can feel stressed when everyone is rushing to get things done or make it out the door. But that doesn't mean you can't take a few seconds to offer descriptive praise.

Let's say you want to see improvements in the morning routine as children get ready for school. You are now in the mindset to notice the good things your child has done instead of focusing on the behavior you want to correct. Those "good things" may be small, but that's okay. Whenever your child gets any of the processes right, use descriptive praise to tell them what desired actions they displayed.

If part of the morning routine didn't go as hoped, just focus on the parts that did go well and pair those prosocial behaviors with descriptive praise. Here are some examples of descriptive praise in the home:

> **NOTE:** These examples are geared toward children, but descriptive praise works for any age. We are never too old to hear that we are doing something right!

- "I love how you brushed your teeth thoroughly. You took your time, and you didn't rush through it. Thank you so much."
- "You were very patient with your little brother. That is so kind of you!"
- "I love how, when it was time to wake up, you got right out of bed and started getting dressed. You had a nice voice and said, 'Good morning, Mommy.' Thank you so much."
- "Wow, I'm impressed by how you got up this morning without a reminder and came down to make your own breakfast. I'm blown away by your maturity."
- "I'm so impressed. You put all your homework into your backpack without a single reminder. You helped your sister pack hers, too! You just made my day."
- "I know this meal isn't your favorite thing, but I love how you showed gratitude and are willing to try it. Thank you."

If you are unsure where to use descriptive praise in the home, think about your morning, daytime, or evening routines. Where are the bottlenecks? When do you feel stress or tension? Think about the small moments, such as getting dressed, eating breakfast, tying shoes, and feeding the dog. What parts of your household routine would benefit from descriptive praise? Write them down here (e.g., brushing teeth, putting dirty clothes away, cleaning the kitchen):

Target those areas that are typically a struggle, then catch your child doing something good. Offer descriptive praise to let them know precisely why you are pleased.

DESCRIPTIVE PRAISE IN THE CLASSROOM

Descriptive praise works well in the classroom, especially since it only takes a few seconds to deliver the accolades and reinforce the desired behavior. Here are a few examples to apply in a classroom setting, regardless of the grade or population of students you teach:

- "I love how you went right to your cubby, got out your worksheet, and sat right down."
- "Wow, you are standing quietly beside your friend, and you've got nice hands down. I love it!"
- "Thank you so much for throwing that piece of trash away. That really helps me."
- "You went straight to the locker room, and your friends followed behind you. Thank you for leading by example. It's a huge help."
- "I love how you threw away your lunch scraps in the trash. You displayed maturity and made things easier for the cleanup crew. Thank you."
- "I noticed you chose to keep your head down during class and not whisper to other students during our test. I'm impressed."

If you are an educator, what classroom behaviors need work? If you are a parent, what behaviors have teachers noticed that would benefit from descriptive praise? Write the behaviors here (e.g., raising hands, listening, throwing trash away, sharing with classmates, being quiet during an exam):

DESCRIPTIVE PRAISE IN THE COMMUNITY

When we walk out the door, the world is waiting. And it's not a very patient or forgiving place at times. Descriptive praise encourages behavior that can make life more joyful and peaceful. It also helps caregivers when our loved ones start to display more prosocial behavior. Here are some examples of descriptive praise outside the home and classroom:

- "I love how you're walking nicely next to the shopping cart. You've got your nice hands down and staying next to me the whole time."
- "Thank you for being so safe in the parking lot. You've got my hand, keeping your hand on the cart and being so slow and cautious."
- "I love how you're trying to put your seatbelt on yourself. I know buckles are hard, and I can help you, but trying it yourself first is so awesome."
- "I'm so proud of you for mowing Mr. Wilson's lawn because he's not well enough to get outside right now. What a kind and helpful young man you have become."
- "You saw the grocery list on the fridge and took the initiative to pick up those items while you were out. You just made my week, and your maturity blows me away."
- "I love that when you asked for help at the store, you said, 'Please.' The world needs more kindness, and you just displayed that. Thank you."

Do you dread going out with your loved one because of certain behaviors? What public behaviors would benefit from your use of descriptive praise? Write the behaviors here (e.g., keeping hands to themselves, not reaching for items on the shelf, being polite to staff):

Descriptive praise reinforces the behaviors that create a more peaceful environment. And who doesn't want that? Just be sure your praise embodies two things:

1. **Sincere Gratitude.** In many ways, gratitude is the missing key to a joyful life. Descriptive praise should include sincere appreciation. By demonstrating gratitude for big and small things, you develop (and model) a heart of thanksgiving. Before you know it, your loved ones will imitate your positivity.

2. **Sincere Truth.** Always be truthful; only offer praise for behaviors that impressed or made you smile. If their behavior makes the home or classroom more peaceful and productive, praise them for it—over and over again.

Descriptive praise changes how you give feedback across multiple environments and increases the likelihood of desired behaviors. Your goal is to foster prosocial behavior—so find the good, describe it, show gratitude, and give praise.

In Brightville, Ethan's parents learned that acknowledging specific behaviors with sincere and detailed praise impacted their child's development. They realized that nurturing a loved one's self-esteem through positive reinforcement was a key to unlocking their confidence and potential.

I encourage you to lay on the praise! Describe how your loved one can please you as you witness their behavior. You're one step closer to experiencing a behavior breakthrough!

Before we move on to the next strategy, you'll have a chance to practice each behavioral skill you just learned. Turn the page to apply descriptive praise to your environment!

APPLICATION EXERCISE

Descriptive Praise

INSTRUCTIONS

Think of a specific behavior or action you want to reinforce. It could be related to academics, chores, social skills, or any other behavioral response. Write the behavior in the space provided below.

Here is an example to get you started: *"I noticed how you took the initiative to clean up your toys without being reminded. That shows responsibility and helps keep our space neat and organized. Great job!"*

BEHAVIOR TO REINFORCE

Example: *Cleaning up toys after playtime*

Now, imagine yourself in a situation where the desired behavior occurs. Fill in the blanks with descriptive and specific praise that you would use to reinforce the behavior. Be detailed and highlight what you specifically noticed about the behavior.

Now, it's your turn. Write the descriptive praise for the behavior you chose.

DESCRIPTIVE PRAISE

By completing this exercise, you can apply descriptive praise to real-life scenarios, hopefully making it easier to alter your language. Create descriptive praise statements to reinforce your understanding as you apply this powerful technique to your daily life.

This book is filled with DO strategies rather than a list of DON'TS. That's because telling people what to do is much more effective than giving them a list of things to stop doing. Once they know how to rise to the occasion, they will!

BEHAVIORAL SKILL 2

Stating Things Positively

The teens and young adults of Brightville weren't immune to the behavioral issues troubling the town. Fourteen-year-old Jacob loved adventure. However, Jacob's parents, the O'Connells, were facing a challenge; they found it increasingly difficult to communicate effectively with their adventurous son.

One early evening, just before dinner, Jacob was headed out the door again without permission. Just then, Mrs. Emerson paid a visit to the O'Connells. They had heard about her remarkable strategies to handle more perplexing behaviors. They hoped she could help them bridge the gap with their teen.

Mrs. Emerson sat down with Jacob and his parents to discuss their concerns. Mr. O'Connell sighed and said, "Jacob, you're always going out with your friends without telling us where you're going. It makes us worried. You never listen to our rules."

With a gentle smile, Mrs. Emerson leaned forward and said, "I know we've discussed descriptive praise.

Now, I'd like to share a behavioral skill with you called 'stating things positively.' Instead of saying, 'You never listen to our rules,' you could try saying, 'Jacob, we appreciate your social nature, but for your safety, let's talk about checking in with us before you head out.'"

Mr. O'Connell looked intrigued and nodded, while Mrs. O'Connell added, "Yes, and instead of saying, 'You're always going out without telling us,' we could say, 'Jacob, we admire your independence, and we want to make sure you're safe when you're out with your friends. Let's work together on some communication guidelines.'"

Jacob's face softened as he listened and thought about Mrs. Emerson's suggestions and how minor word changes can have a big impact.

With Mrs. Emerson's guidance, the O'Connells practiced this new way of communication. They began using positively worded statements to address Jacob's outings, carefully describing what Jacob should do instead of what he shouldn't do or what irritated his parents. They found that Jacob responded more openly, and they could have constructive conversations about his social adventures.

Over time, Jacob felt more understood and appreciated by his parents and, with his parents' guidance, he continued to explore Brightville's wonders while keeping them informed about his plans. The power of stating things positively brought harmony to their household, showing that even the most adventurous teenagers can thrive when their loved ones communicate in a way that provides a path to desired behaviors.

We all know the saying, "It's not what you say but how you say it." It's age-old wisdom that highlights 1) the power of our communication style and 2) the impact that tone and clarity can have on the results. This principle is especially true for parents, educators, and adults who are responsible for guiding loved ones and learners.

But there's more to it than just the delivery of your words. The next skill goes a step further. It's about focusing on what you want to see (prosocial behaviors) rather than dwelling on what you don't (problematic behaviors). The "stating things positively" approach involves more than being optimistic; it's a practical way to shape behavior and encourage more of the actions and attitudes you want to see. You'll see how this technique fits seamlessly into everyday communication and can transform how you guide and teach.

ESSENTIALS
The Basics of Stating Things Positively

Stating things positively sounds so easy, doesn't it? And it is—with a catch. It unlocks the true power of communication. While paying attention to *how* you say something is vital, choosing the *exact words* to help guide behavior and reinforce the right things is even more important. Words have the unique ability to shape the way people think and act. Imagine if you could use words to inspire more constructive actions and behaviors. That's the essence of stating things positively.

STATING THINGS POSITIVELY

A behavioral skill where you express thoughts, requests, or rules by focusing on what you want to happen instead of what you want to avoid or stop

Stating things positively is like using a superpower for desired behavior. By emphasizing a goal (the prosocial behavior you want to see), you motivate your loved one to comply. Here's a simple example: Instead of saying, "Don't make a mess," try saying, "Please keep the toys at the table only, and before getting up, place them back into their bins."

Can you see how stating things positively is a good thing? Positive statements are easy to agree with, yet most people speak negatively all day—to themselves and others. Why? Because our brains have a built-in "negativity bias." That means we pay more attention to bad or potentially harmful things.

In the ancient past, an awareness of danger helped our ancestors survive. Over time, this habit of seeing danger around every corner became a mental safety mechanism.

However, in today's world, focusing on negativity can lead to interpersonal problems, impacting behavior in an undesired way. For instance, when you repeatedly point out how badly someone has messed up or disobeyed, you probably get pushback. The person might shut you out or shut down entirely.

That's why it's time for some wording changes.

Any time you ask someone else to do something that may be aversive or challenging, your choice of words is impactful. When you state things positively, you tell people what to *do* instead of what *not* to do. In other words, you give them a plan of action rather than point out potential wrongs (which may spark ideas or displays of problematic behavior).

Stating things positively highlights the solution (helpful) instead of the problem (not helpful).

Simply pointing out the problem behaviors or saying, "Stop!" or "Don't do that!" is frustrating—and ineffective. Whenever you draw attention to unwanted behavior, you focus on that problem, not the solution.

For example, think about what a student hears when you say, "Stop spitting on the ground." They hear "stop," and then they hear "spitting." The focus is on the challenging behavior. Not good! They will likely continue spitting if there's a history of opposition or noncompliance.

> This technique is especially powerful for people with a history of opposition or non-compliance. It is also helpful for people who struggle to respect requests from authority figures.

"No" and "stop" can also be trigger words for some learners. By focusing on criticism, you set yourself up for a power struggle.

To state things positively, say this instead: "I'd like you to tell me what you need, then keep your mouth closed as I help you and the other students."

That response accomplishes far more than merely telling the student to stop spitting. You help the student focus on the correct behavior (asking for help and then keeping their mouth closed). You also help them understand that spitting is incompatible with a closed mouth.

Tell them precisely what you want them to do. Then, take it a step further and give them something to do instead (because if they are talking to you, it will be difficult for them to continue spitting).

What if siblings are fighting over a toy and hitting each other rather than sharing? Typically, parents shout, "Stop!" In that case, the children hear a negatively charged word rather than hearing the behavior their parent wants to see. Instead of saying, "Stop," the parent should say, "Please put your hands to your sides and step apart."

The children now know what behaviors they need to display. As a result, the parent can help them find an appropriate solution.

Tell your children what to *do* instead of what *not* to do. That is stating your request positively.

REASONING
Why Stating Things Positively Works

Constantly criticizing and using phrases like "no," "stop," and "I don't like that" not only fails to provide solutions but also fills conversations with needless criticism. This constant focus on problematic behavior can lead loved ones and learners to become more critical of themselves and others.

When you continually provide feedback that identifies and labels problems, you risk becoming your child's inner voice of criticism, which can later translate to low self-esteem.

On the other hand, when you guide with directives, explaining the advantages of engaging in prosocial behaviors, you're more likely to receive cooperation. This approach promotes communication because it is built on problem-solving, love, and care. It nurtures relationships that are grounded in mutual respect. It also encourages compromise, negotiation, and open conversation, enabling everyone to work together effectively.

By stating things positively, you build a relationship based on productive interactions, leading to trust and enjoyment, not nagging and avoidance.

Changing your wording might sound like a small thing, but it can make a world of difference in increasing prosocial behavior. When you talk to our loved ones and learners this way:

- **You make things clear.** Stating things positively leaves no room for confusion. Your loved ones and those in your care know what you expect from them. They can now meet your expectations without guesswork.

- **You give them power.** Stating things positively makes those around you feel like superheroes. They get to choose to do the right thing, and that's pretty cool. We all enjoy being around people who make it easy for us to be successful.

- **You get their cooperation.** When you state things positively, those in your care are more likely to listen and do what you ask without a fuss.

- **You build strong bonds.** Stating things positively helps everyone get along better. You build trust, especially since nobody likes to argue.

By shifting your focus from constant criticism to constructive counsel, you can help your loved ones and learners develop a healthy self-image and valuable people skills. So, choose positivity as your language of connection and growth.

APPLICATION
Stating Things Positively in Action

It's time to use stating things positively in a few examples so you can apply them to your home or classroom situations.

STATING THINGS POSITIVELY IN THE HOME

Let's say a child is running around, creating a disruption, or doing something unsafe. If you yell, "No!" or "Calm down!" you are not addressing the problem. You haven't provided clear expectations (what they should do instead). Therefore, you're less likely to get an effective response. Try this instead:

- "I need you to stop moving your feet. Now use slow turtle walking feet."

What if you are headed to the library with your children? They will need to be quiet and not disrupt others. Before you walk in, you could say, "No yelling, running, hitting, or spitting," but those words put the focus on the undesired behaviors. You are highlighting the problems, not the solution. Instead, tell them what you want to see. Say something like this:

- "When we are in the library, I want everyone to keep their hands to themselves. I want your voices in a whisper. You will stay near me while I look at my books first, and then we will go to the children's section, where you may look at your books. We'll each find one book to check out. And once you have found your book to check out, I want you to sit on the couch and wait for me. Then we will all check out together."

Stating things positively works well for teens, too (we're never too old to learn the right thing to do). Teenagers may use certain tones and language their parents and teachers find disrespectful. A parent or teacher may say in response to an undesired tone, "You are not allowed to talk to me like that. You're being very disrespectful." With this statement, you are drawing attention to all the things the teen should not be doing. How about this instead:

- "I see that you are upset about something. I understand and respect that. I want us to discuss this situation in a calm and quiet voice. Let's talk to each other respectfully. That way, I can try to help you solve your problem, and we can communicate with kind words."

If they are playing loud music in their room, don't yell, "It's too loud! You're giving me a headache!" Instead, try this:

- "I'd prefer you to play your music on a lower level. If you set the volume between three and five, it's more pleasant for your family."

Tell your loved ones what you want to see! They will respond much better to instruction than critique.

STATING THINGS POSITIVELY
IN THE CLASSROOM

Let's apply this skill to the classroom. Suppose the students aren't keeping their hands to themselves during carpet time. They pick at each other's clothing, play with each other's hair, and touch other peers, causing a disruption. Stating the correction ineffectively could sound like, "I need everyone to stop." But that doesn't tell the learners what to do, and it's less likely to get the desired response. Instead, state things positively:

- "I need everyone to have their hands in their laps. Now, touch your nose, touch your head, and sit on your hands."

During lunch, let's say a child shows peers chewed food in their mouth. Stating things ineffectively may sound like, "Stop, that's disgusting!" But that doesn't offer a problem-solving solution. Tell them what to do instead:

- "Please chew with your mouth closed and swallow your food before you open your mouth."

One of your students is scribbling on their paper, not using their best handwriting, and you know they can do better. You could say, "Quit scribbling. That is not good handwriting." But why not try this:

- "Please set your pencil down and use your big eraser to erase the marks that are not your best handwriting. Then pick your pencil up and try again using your most careful, best handwriting."

Now, let's say a teacher overhears an older student complaining about them ("Mrs. Smith is so unfair!" or "Mr. Jones always picks on me."). The teacher could say, "That's not how you solve problems with someone. It's hurtful to talk about me or anyone behind their backs." But then you've just labeled the problem and accused the student of being hurtful, which is unproductive. Instead, say:

- "You're upset with me, which is your right. Next time, you are welcome to discuss it with me. I want to learn and grow, so if you tell me what I'm doing that's upsetting you, we can fix it together."

Tell people what you want to see. Give your loved ones or learners the roadmap to a successful, peaceful trip, day, classroom, or home environment! Parents, teachers, and anyone working with young people can state things positively in everyday situations. Here are a few other examples:

GOAL	INEFFECTIVE FEEDBACK	STATING THINGS POSITIVELY
Set Rules	"No running inside."	"Let's walk indoors."
Handle Changes	"Don't take forever to get ready."	"Let's get dressed by 7:55 a.m. so we have more playtime."
Increase Effort	"You're not trying hard enough.	"Use your slow handwriting and keep your letters on the lines."
Express Disagreement	"Quit arguing."	"I like when you express your ideas in a nice voice, but when we disagree, we can each share what we want and compromise to give each other a little of what we want."

Encourage Healthy Eating	"Don't eat so much junk food."	"Let's choose one serving of chips and then one fresh fruit."
Promote Safety	"Stop being so reckless. You're going to get hurt."	"Stop at the stop sign, count to five, and look both ways."
Manage Screen Time	"You're always on the iPad!"	"Set the timer for twenty minutes; when it sounds, we can select another activity together."
Help with Forgetfulness	"You never remember anything!"	"Let's put a note by the backdoor to help us remember when it's trash day."

Over in Brightville, Jacob's growing connection with his parents became evident. Their support and guidance helped him safely navigate his adventures and fostered a sense of understanding and appreciation within their family. This transformation underscored the impact of stating things positively, demonstrating its ability to bring harmony and enable even the most adventurous youth to flourish.

Stating things positively is like a secret recipe for excellent behavior. It defines the desired behavior, leaves no room for confusion, and ensures that nagging and avoidance are no longer a part of your relationships. It's a friendly, productive way to guide others in the right direction. You can use this superpower to help those around you grow, learn, and feel fantastic about themselves.

APPLICATION EXERCISE

Stating Things Positively

INSTRUCTIONS

Let's keep this exercise simple because this strategy is simple. Choose an alternative response for the following examples. Replace the ineffective comment about undesired behavior with a clear statement that tells the child what kind of behavior you want to see.

EXAMPLE

Ineffective feedback: "You never listen to me when I'm talking. You're so disrespectful."

Stating things positively: "I appreciate it when you actively engage in our conversations and tell me what you need. It helps us to connect better."

PRACTICE

Ineffective feedback: "You're always late, and it's so annoying."

Stating things positively:

Ineffective feedback: "You're so messy and lazy. Why don't you ever clean up after yourself?"

Stating things positively:

Ineffective feedback: "Stop playing video games all day. You're wasting your life away."

Stating things positively:

BONUS CONTENT EXAMPLE

GOAL	INEFFECTIVE FEEDBACK	STATING THINGS POSITIVELY
Improve Listening Skills	"Pay attention! Stop yelling!"	"Voices off, eyes on me, and listening ears."
Be a Kinder Friend	"You're too wild! Get out of their faces! They don't like that!"	"Take a step back, keep your hands at your sides, use your words to say, 'Do you want to play tag?'"
Complete a Task	"No! You're not done yet!"	"Please return to your bedroom, check the floor for toys, and ensure that each one is placed in the right basket."
Stay Focused	"Stop bouncing around!"	"Keep your eyes on the book, remain seated with a quiet voice, and read to page 25."

Experiencing a Behavior Breakthrough means knowing how to impact your child's environment. You respond consistently, and you encourage your child to exhibit more prosocial behavior. The next step is learning when to offer incentives.

BEHAVIORAL SKILL 3

Delivering Preferred Outcomes

In the Brightville suburbs, a young girl named Lily Anderson would get lost in her imagination. She often dreamed that she was the captain of a pirate ship and would spend hours at the local park, swaying wildly on the swings as though she were being tossed around on the high seas.

But lately, Lily had found it challenging to control her emotions and manage her behavior. Because of that, her parents found it hard to take Lily to the park (or anywhere, for that matter). Mr. and Mrs. Anderson recognized the shift in her behavior, so they sought guidance from the beloved Mrs. Emerson.

Mrs. Emerson knew it was time to tell the Andersons about a therapeutic approach called "delivering preferred outcomes." She explained that they had done well implementing descriptive praise and stating things positively. So, it was time to continue building on key behavioral skills to help Lily. That meant they needed to start delivering preferred outcomes, but only at the correct times.

Intrigued by the concept, Mr. and Mrs. Anderson learned more about using preferred outcomes to support Lily's growth. They realized that by providing incentives tied to specific behaviors, they could encourage Lily to develop healthier habits and make better choices.

With Mrs. Emerson's guidance, the Andersons began using preferred outcomes. They involved Lily in the process, allowing her to occasionally select her preferred outcomes or rewards when she exhibited prosocial behavior. They even created a list of desired behaviors they wished to see more of.

Every time Lily accomplished one of these goals, her parents would celebrate her achievement by offering an outcome they knew she loved. It could be anything from a special outing to her favorite ice cream place, extra playtime, a small toy she had been eyeing, or reading or game time with her parents.

One warm afternoon, the Andersons noticed Lily practicing patience while waiting for her turn on the swing at the park. Overjoyed by her progress, they praised her effort and delivered a preferred outcome of fifteen extra minutes of playtime. She became more aware that good things happened when she made prosocial choices. Her parents' consistency helped Lily make this important connection.

Encouraged by these positive outcomes, Lily's behavior continued to improve. She tackled her homework with renewed focus and commitment, kept her room tidy without reminders, and displayed greater self-control in challenging situations. Delivering preferred outcomes became a powerful motivator for Lily, helping her build resilience and self-discipline. She also learned that problematic behaviors did not allow her to obtain the outcomes she wished for most.

Lily's parents discovered that timing mattered. By delivering preferred outcomes at the right time, they could focus on prosocial behavior rather than reinforcing undesired behavior. The Andersons witnessed their daughter's growth into a responsible, self-assured, and compassionate young lady. Their confidence as parents also grew, ensuring they delivered preferred outcomes only after Lily demonstrated desired behaviors.

When dealing with behavioral issues, few things are more satisfying than witnessing tangible progress. The Andersons felt optimistic and excited after seeing the changes this strategy could make—and you can feel that kind of excitement, too! Implementing the behavioral skill in this chapter will empower others to unlock their potential. You can reinforce desired behaviors by awarding preferred outcomes at the proper time. So, let's dive in.

ESSENTIALS
The Basics of Delivering Preferred Outcomes

The concept of delivering preferred outcomes is simple but powerful. By reinforcing prosocial behaviors, people begin to make meaningful—and lasting—changes to their conduct. Delivering desired outcomes is a powerful way to assert environmental control and produce more behaviors you want to see. Let's define the strategy more clearly:

DELIVERING PREFERRED OUTCOMES

A strategy that grants access to enjoyable consequences when appropriate behavior is displayed

When you deliver a preferred outcome to a loved one or learner, you make something available to them that you know they love. But the catch is this: you grant access contingent (dependent) upon their display of a desired behavior.

You are aware of the *delivery timing* of good things, ensuring that a desired behavior has happened *first*. Prosocial behavior must come right before the delivery of good things in life!

Delivering preferred outcomes is *not* the same as reinforcement. Displaying a desired behavior results in good things. That is true in every area of life! What a valuable lesson to teach a loved one.

You can provide a preferred outcome by giving your attention or granting access to something they enjoy. Or you can take away something aversive. Either way, you have the power to deliver a preferred outcome.

TAKING AWAY SOMETHING
AS A PREFERRED OUTCOME?

Preferred outcomes don't have to be prizes, toys, or attention. You can also remove things that aren't enjoyable.

Imagine that your son wants to watch his favorite TV show but can't until he puts his toys away. He's not too excited about cleaning up, and it feels a bit aversive (unpleasant) because he'd rather be watching TV. Nevertheless, he responds calmly and agrees to clean up.

Here's how you take away something aversive (cleaning up the toys) to give you the power to deliver a preferred outcome (not having to clean up the toys at all or right away). You say:

> "I know you're unhappy about cleaning up your toys. However, I love how you kept a quiet and calm voice when I asked you to clean up, and you still agreed! As a result of your good attitude, you can skip cleaning your toys for now, and we can clean together after dinner."

In this example, taking away toy cleanup (aversive task), even for a short while, is a way to deliver a preferred outcome to increase the likelihood of having a good attitude when asked to clean up in the future.

If you are a caregiver, think how you would feel if someone told you, "Don't worry about doing the morning

---

routine today. I'll take care of it! I'll get the children dressed, make breakfast, pack their bags, ensure that homework is signed and completed, and get them set for the day!" Taking away a demanding activity or something not always enjoyable can be just as satisfying as receiving a preferred activity or item.

In behavioral terms, this is using negative reinforcement (taking away the aversive task of cleaning up) to encourage a preferred behavior (quiet voice and agreeable behavior) to increase the future frequency of the desired behavior.

Delivering preferred outcomes is based on the principles of *operant conditioning*. It's a concept in psychology that explains how behavior is learned and changed. It may sound like a complex term, but operant conditioning merely suggests that you can modify behaviors through positive reinforcement (giving something) and negative reinforcement (taking something away).

When people learn certain desired outcomes in their environment, they will likely repeat the behaviors that led to those results. So, to encourage prosocial behavior, you must ensure that you only deliver preferred outcomes as a direct result of seeing the desired behaviors.

It's your job to ensure that preferred outcomes occur *after* appropriate behavior (and are therefore seen as a direct consequence of that desired behavior).

When you deliver preferred outcomes as a response to undesired, disruptive behaviors, you will see more of those same challenging behaviors. Here's what that could look like:

- Your child cries, so you give him another juice box.
- Your son throws a tantrum in the grocery store, so you buy him a toy to quiet him down.
- Your daughter refuses to help clean up after dinner, so you send her to her room, where she has unrestricted access to her phone and social media.

When you do this, you signal to your child, "Cry/get upset/act defiantly, and I will get what I want." That's why it's important to be purposeful in delivering preferred outcomes only after the desired behavior (and not when you're at your wit's end and just want the undesired behavior to stop).

Since the timing of the preferred outcomes is key, focus on the right timing. For example, let's say your child has unrestricted access to their toy basket, no matter their behavior. They just displayed a behavior you don't prefer (they took their snack to the couch after you asked them to keep it at the kitchen table) and then accessed their favorite basket of toys. Because of their ability to access those toys (a preferred outcome) after that undesired behavior, that could potentially reinforce (increase) the undesired behavior that occurred immediately prior.

Once you become aware of preferred outcome timing, you know to deliver the preferred basket of toys only *after* they display a desired behavior. Such delivery timing is purposeful and allows for environmental contingencies that might reinforce appropriate behaviors.

REASONING
Why Delivering Preferred Outcomes Works

If you're like most parents or educators, you are in the habit of delivering preferred outcomes whenever a child asks for them. When you provide something preferred upon request, you reinforce that your child or student can ask for what they want and get it, regardless of their behavior. That may be helpful if functional communication is a challenge for them. But if communication is not a skill you are targeting at that moment, you might rethink your approach.

When you provide preferred outcomes too freely, children learn they can get what they want by demanding it, crying, or throwing a tantrum.

Asking for what you want is important; we all need to know how to ask for things. However, delivering preferred outcomes serves a different purpose. It's a tool that says:

"I know that my child wants this thing. Since they've shown an interest in it in the past, I will use it as a reward. Instead of waiting for them to ask for the item (or privilege, etc.), I will give it to them freely when I see a desired behavior. That way, my child learns that prosocial behavior results in preferred outcomes."

Delivering things when loved ones and students ask for them is still acceptable, but it's even better when you get ahead of the requests and use their preferred choices to improve behavior.

You're the one in control of the environment. Don't forget that.

But this raises an interesting question: Is delivering preferred outcomes the same as bribing your child? Delivering preferred outcomes and bribing a child seem similar because both involve offering something to encourage specific behavior. However, there are important distinctions between the two:

Delivering Preferred Outcomes:

- Seeks to increase behaviors that are already expected or desired.
- Rewards (known preferences) are given in response to appropriate behavior or effort.
- Focuses on long-term results, turning desirable behavior into a habit.
- Is used consistently.
- Recognizes that reinforcement is part of a larger strategy to support development and learning.

Bribery:

- Seeks to use rewards as a stopgap to get instant compliance.
- Rewards children without planning to control inappropriate behavior.
- Focuses on short-term results or getting the child to do something specific "right now."
- Is often used inconsistently and impulsively.
- Is often a shortcut to avoid addressing underlying issues.

Bribes can lead to unfortunate consequences. They promote undesired behavior when a child gets their way through whining, demanding, crying, screaming, or acting out. In contrast, delivering preferred outcomes supports desired behavior. When you start to see more desired behavior, you know that providing a known preference is working!

APPLICATION
Delivering Preferred Outcomes in Action

Follow these steps to ensure that you're delivering preferred outcomes in a way that increases the frequency of desired behavior in the future. It's important to note that a preferred outcome for one person may not appeal to someone else. While I may find chores aversive and be motivated by their removal, someone else may enjoy mopping or pushing a heavy vacuum for sensory reasons. It's best to take an individualized approach.

Delivering preferred outcomes involves these simple steps:

1. Identify target behaviors.

What specific behaviors do you want to encourage or change? That includes both sides of the behavior spectrum: the prosocial skills you want to see developed and undesired behaviors you want to decrease. The desired behavior you seek creates a more peaceful and joyful environment for them, you, and everyone else affected.

2. Identify preferred outcomes.

Evaluate what outcomes your loved one or learner enjoys. Be as specific as possible. Create a list of preferred outcomes. Don't just list their favorite things. Include lower-level outcomes that are still enjoyable. Identifying both the most desired outcomes *and* the lower-level preferred outcomes allows you to be aware of delivering access to any desired outcomes (and avoid inadvertently reinforcing an undesired behavior).

3. Deal preferred outcomes only *after* desired behaviors.

It's your job to deliver preferred outcomes immediately after the child exhibits the desired behavior. By reinforcing the prosocial behavior, the child is more likely to repeat it.

4. Monitor and adjust.

Monitor the child's progress and adjust the plan as needed. Some preferred outcomes may serve as effective reinforcers, and some may not. Track behavioral progress by looking at behavioral trends. If problem behaviors are happening less frequently, you may be able to conclude that you are delivering preferred outcomes appropriately.

> **The best way to ensure effectiveness is to become a data collector. You can review patterns of behavior in many ways.**

Accurately collecting data involves gathering information about a person's behavior, preferences, strengths, and areas of improvement. This data-driven approach allows for a better understanding of individual needs and helps tailor the delivery of preferred outcomes. Here are some methods for collecting relevant data:

- **Observation:** Pay attention to the child's responses to different situations and interactions with others. Don't gauge reactions; just gauge their responses. Sometimes, your loved one's responses won't correspond with behavioral trends, and that's okay. You just care about the data and what it tells you.

- **Direct conversations:** Ask about their interests, likes, dislikes, and specific behaviors they want to improve, then list them. You can also collaborate with your loved one and their educators and caregivers to create this list.

- **Feedback and Self-Reporting:** Encourage the child to provide feedback on their progress and how they feel about the preferred outcomes and rewards they receive. However, remember that data collected from your direct observations is the most telling.

- **Collaboration:** Work closely with teachers, parents, and other professionals involved in the child's care to share and integrate data.

- **Data Recording:** Keep track of behaviors and responses over time. That could involve behavior charts, ABC (Antecedent, Behavior, Consequence) recording, or other data-collection methods. Use this data collection to observe overall behavioral trends to evaluate progress.

The right data helps you decide if delivering preferred outcomes impacts behavior change in a desired way.

5. Maintain awareness of preferred outcomes.

From the beginning, you should see the effect of certain behavioral changes. Continue to monitor the child's behavior, including undesired behavior. When you see desired behavior (big or small), deliver preferred outcomes. Remember that rewards are contingent on desired behavior. Your awareness can impact the child's environment and help reduce the incidences of problem behaviors.

6. Generalize the lessons.

The bigger life goal is for your loved one or learner to apply prosocial behaviors in various settings and environments. Generalizing the lessons can help ensure that desired changes persist in everyday life (across settings and people). Are fewer problem behaviors occurring after you deliver preferred outcomes (and only at the appropriate times)? If the answer is YES, you know you are using an effective strategy.

While you can't measure or collect data everywhere, generalization occurs when our loved ones or learners transfer their improved behavior trends to school, a relative's home, a play date, when hanging out with friends, or during a sporting event.

Remember, delivering preferred outcomes isn't about providing those in your care with certain items or activities that are rare and extra special; it is about being aware of preferred *everyday* events and ensuring that the desired behavior occurs *before* you grant access.

DELIVERING PREFERRED OUTCOMES IN THE HOME

Being purposeful and ensuring that you deliver preferred outcomes at the right time will significantly impact your child's desire to repeat the desired behaviors that happened right before. So, let's break it down and provide a few examples.

Let's say you are working with a toddler on increasing functional communication and decreasing tantrum behaviors to communicate their wants and needs, especially with food. A desired outcome for a toddler might be their preferred snack of apple slices. So, you deliver this snack any time the toddler displays a functional communication response regarding food.

- If they say "more" instead of crying, give them their desired outcome (the apple slice) and reinforce with descriptive praise, as in, "Yay, nice job saying, 'More.' You can have another apple slice."

- If your toddler walks over to the pantry and points to the snacks, reward this behavior with the apple slices as a replacement for tantrums or crying. Then say, "Yes, good! Thank you for showing Mommy where the snacks are stored. Now you can have more snacks."

Always follow up with descriptive praise so there are no doubts about what caused you to deliver the preferred outcome.

Let's say you want your school-aged child to complete their homework without whining, negotiating, or other problem behaviors. When you witness them sitting at your dining room table, working on their homework (or they respond correctly to a homework question), deliver a preferred outcome.

- "Hey, let's go take a ten-minute break. You get to watch TV, or you can spend ten minutes on your iPad."

- "You're working so hard on your homework. Would you like an extra slice of grandma's pie?"

It's vital to notice the good in the environment and ensure that you deliver a preferred outcome the moment your child displays a desired behavior that changes the environment.

Maybe your teen usually retreats to their bedroom when they come home, but tonight, they are conversing with the family. Immediately allow access to a desired outcome:

- "I love that you are spending time with your family tonight. This weekend, would you like to go to the mall? Or would you like to have a friend over?"

DELIVERING PREFERRED OUTCOMES IN THE CLASSROOM

Now, let's discuss delivering preferred outcomes in a group setting. Let's say you are working on having students request to use the restroom before it becomes too late and someone has an accident. When you see a student asking to use the restroom, deliver that preferred outcome. Say something like this:

- "Good job listening to your body and asking to use the potty. Here are some goldfish crackers."
- "I'm proud of you for using the bathroom like a big kid. You can sit on my lap during circle time while we read."

Perhaps you want to increase the desired behavior of students raising their hands without blurting out. When a student raises their hand, you respond:

- "Thank you so much for raising your hand and waiting with your voice off. I would love to hear what you have to say."
- You may also reward them with free time to draw, a few extra minutes at recess, or allow them to be the teacher's helper.

Let's say a student helps a peer who is having trouble with an assignment. Let's also say that the struggling student is socially isolated. You love seeing the helpful student demonstrate kindness and patience. So, you decide to deliver a desired outcome to that student for displaying appropriate social skills, especially by reaching out to a student who needs it most. So, you take the student aside and say:

- "I saw you helping Taylor, and I know it meant a lot to him. I want you to hang out here for a little bit and help me like you loved doing last week. Let me get you a hall pass so you can stay."
- "You can spend some extra time on the iPad this afternoon. I saw you helping Taylor. It was mature and kind, making my day and his!"

To decrease problem behaviors in any environment, target the desired behaviors you see and purposefully deliver desired outcomes. Just remember that classroom-based preferred outcomes follow the same rule as home-based strategies. They must be individualized for each child.

That is how behavior change happens.

Providing desired rewards is a powerful way to encourage desired behavior and create a nurturing atmosphere, particularly for people like Lucy in Brightville.

By customizing their approach to her interests and requirements, Lucy's parents used preferred rewards and incentives to spark improvements in her behavior. These rewards not only made Lucy feel a sense of achievement but also enhanced her bond with her parents, establishing trust and promoting open communication.

Delivering preferred outcomes contingent upon your child's desired behaviors can create a ripple effect, extending beyond their home life and into their school and interactions with the world.

As caregivers, educators, and supporters, we should deliver preferred outcomes only *after* a loved one or learner demonstrates appropriate behavior. By doing so, we help to build a world where children and young adults thrive and grow. We provide the encouragement and guidance they need. As a result, those around us will find joy as they reach their full potential. Indeed, small mindset changes and a focus on the environment can spark extraordinary transformations in the hearts and minds of our loved ones.

APPLICATION EXERCISE

Delivering Preferred Outcomes

Comprehension Check! Fill in the blanks (Answers at the bottom of the page):

Preferred outcomes require me to be aware of times when I deliver something "good" or enjoyable and to avoid accidentally_____problem behaviors. I should be mindful of the outcomes I deliver and their environments to ensure that_____behavior happens first.

Answer Key: 1. reinforcing 2. desired

Use this table to begin recording 1) desired behaviors you want to see, 2) everyday preferred outcomes that could result from a display of those desired behaviors, and 3) behaviors that do not justify preferred outcomes.

DESIRED BEHAVIORS THAT JUSTIFY A PREFERRED OUTCOME	COMMON PREFERRED OUTCOMES ALREADY IN MY ENVIRONMENT	PROBLEM BEHAVIORS THAT DO NOT JUSTIFY A PREFERRED OUTCOME

FIRST, you read and digest this book. THEN, you have a repertoire of behavioral skills to help you focus on the right goals to see more desired behavior! In other words...

FIRST, you read this book. THEN, you learn how to experience a behavior breakthrough!

BEHAVIORAL SKILL 4

First/Then Contingency

We find ourselves again in Brightville, where Alex Garcia was known for his boundless energy and enthusiasm. However, his impulsive choices often led to challenging behaviors, especially when transitioning from one activity to another. Alex's grandparents were determined to find a way to help Alex navigate transitions more smoothly.

The Garcias had been using descriptive praise and delivering preferred outcomes, and those behavioral skills were helpful. They needed additional guidance, so they again turned to Mrs. Emerson. She told them about a technique called a "first/then contingency." She explained that this approach could provide the structure and support Alex needed during transitions, reducing his resistance and tantrums.

Excited to try it, the Garcias implemented the first/then contingency technique at home. They went as far as to create a visual schedule for Alex, depicting two simple steps for each transition: "first" represented the current task or activity, and "then" indicated the desired activity that would follow.

As Alex played with his toys one morning, his grandma showed him the visual schedule. It read: "First: Clean up toys; Then: Go to the park." By displaying the agenda in a prominent place, Alex could easily refer to it whenever a transition was approaching. The chart also served as a reminder for the Garcias, helping them engage less with Alex during transitions. As a result, his protest behavior decreased.

When it was time to clean up, Alex's grandma pointed to the schedule. "First: Pick up toys; Then: Go to the park." Using "first/then" helped Alex understand the sequence of events and prepared him for the upcoming change. It also provided a preferred outcome for engaging in the transition instead of just receiving a non-preferred request with no hope of receiving anything good.

As they arrived at the park, Alex's grandpa explained, "First, we'll leave the park after a thirty-minute playtime; then, we'll get an ice cream treat!" Typically, Alex threw a tantrum when it was time to leave the park, but this time, his eyes sparkled at the promise of ice cream. The Garcias noted the difference in Alex's behavior. He was more cooperative and appeared excited about the transition, knowing that something enjoyable awaited.

The Garcias continued to use the first/then contingency technique, and in time, they saw Alex's resistance and meltdowns diminish. He began transitioning between activities with less stress and frustration.

One evening, as Alex ate dinner, his grandpa told him, "First, finish your vegetables; then, play a board game with me." Alex's motivation to finish his meal soared, and he eagerly ate his vegetables to get to his fun board game time.

The Garcias were thrilled to see the once-challenging transitions become smoother and more enjoyable for their grandson. The first/then contingency had become an essential part of their toolkit, helping them provide the structure and support Alex needed to thrive.

If you want to see an increase in prosocial behavior and a decrease in undesired behavior (and who wouldn't?), you'll love the first/contingency. Let's explore this incredible tool! Don't worry—we will break it down and normalize it for everyday use (since making ice cream an option after every request is unrealistic). First/then contingencies are not just for transitions or always involve extra special rewards; they're about providing structure.

ESSENTIALS
The Basics of First/Then Contingency

The first/then contingency is simple and effective! There are two steps: 1) you show or explain what needs to happen first, and 2) show or explain what happens after completing that action.

When you use this technique, your loved one or learners will be able to understand the sequence of events, and transitions will be smoother and more manageable.

FIRST/THEN CONTINGENCY

A behavioral technique that involves presenting two steps in sequence: "first" represents the current activity or task, and "then" indicates the preferred or desired activity that will follow after they complete the first one

To be clear, the first activity you present is usually neutrally preferred or aversive/undesirable. But once they complete that activity, they will receive something more desirable.

Generally, the more aversive the "first" activity is, the more desirable the "then" activity needs to be.

If I am going to complete an aversive task, I want to do something I genuinely enjoy—something that is not usually readily available to me. That way, the "then" reward is worth the "first" activity! For example, doing taxes is highly aversive to me. I don't enjoy sitting for long periods, and breaking down budgets or dealing with finances is a form of personal torture. I would not be willing to complete my taxes in one sitting (the "first" activity) if someone promised to take me to Starbucks (a "then" reward). I don't like coffee, so that reward would not motivate me. The promise of a high five wouldn't inspire me, either.

Therefore, completing my taxes in one sitting—an aversive or unpleasant activity—needs to be followed by something I highly prefer. A more appealing "then" activity would be a nap (I don't get too many of those with two young children and a career) or a spa pedicure.

When an aversive activity is followed by an enjoyable one, the child is more likely to participate in the first part because they realize, "I *have* to complete this task, but then I *get* to do what I want."

A key to using this technique effectively is to describe the first/then *before* challenging behaviors have had a chance to occur. Give the child time to understand that they must complete a less desirable task (and do it with prosocial attitudes) to get what they want.

Suppose you offer the first/then contingency *after* the child displays undesired behavior. In that case, you inadvertently reinforce or even increase the future displays of undesired behaviors. (This would be bribing, which we will dissect later in the book).

For example, if your child always cries when it's time to leave the park, don't present the first/then contingency of "First leave the park, then get ice cream" *after* a tantrum is already underway. Instead, offer the first/then contingency once you arrive at the park *before* play begins. Give your child time to adjust to the idea so the undesired behavior doesn't happen. You may also need to remind them of the first/then sequence a few times *during* play (this is especially true for younger children).

The first/then contingency is a *proactive* technique, not a reactive one! It gives those around us a light at the end of the tunnel. That way, they find the motivation to engage in something that is non-preferred or aversive to them.

REASONING
Why the First/Then Contingency Works

Why invest time and energy in communicating first/then contingencies? Because people need to look forward to something good. Knowing that aversive tasks or requests won't last forever is encouraging. And it's highly motivating to learn that a preferred activity comes next!

Independently functioning adults often structure their lives in a first/then contingency fashion. We make hard choices daily when there is the promise of something more preferred later. See if these examples sound familiar to you:

- "First, I'm going for a run; then, I can splurge on a cookie."
- "First, I will complete all the studying for my continuing education course; then, I will shop at TJ Maxx (or eat at my favorite restaurant)."

Since adults instinctively use this structure, providing the same format for children to motivate them makes sense. Our careers also revolve around this idea: "First, I go to work; then, I get a paycheck."

It's not bribery—it's using what we know about the human brain and its response to rewards in order to decrease undesired behavior.

By implementing the first/then contingency, you teach those around you how to organize their lives, tackle activities they may not prefer, and find the motivation to adopt appropriate behavior.

The first/then contingency helps loved ones and learners prioritize tasks and complete the undesirable ones first. By rewarding their obedience, you encourage growth and prosocial behavior.

If undesired behavior occurs, remind the child of the "first" contingency. They must comply with the initial instructions *before* they receive the reward.

First/then contingencies are especially effective for those who make high-frequency requests or demands (lots of questions, needs, and requests over short periods). Do you have a child who asks you 37 questions first thing in the morning? If so, great!

You can provide children like that with a first/then contingency to help them get what they want while, at the same time, you get what you want (you want them to sit down, feed the dog, brush their teeth, finish their breakfast, be kind to their siblings, etc.).

Identify and remember what they want (or even write them down). Now you don't have to wonder what will motivate them to display the desired behavior. Pay attention when your child says something like this:

- "Can I go to my friend's house?"
- "Can I have a snack?"
- "Can I watch TV?"

Use requests like these as your "then" contingencies. Here is an example:

Child: "Can I get on my computer for a bit?"

Parent: "Sure. But first, I need you to clean up your room; then, you may get on your computer."

What's going to happen after an exchange like this? A few things: 1) you'll increase compliance, 2) you'll increase the motivation to complete less desirable tasks, and 3) you'll decrease high-frequency requests. Respond to your child's repeated request by asking them to complete an aversive task. Win-win-win!

APPLICATION
First/Then Contingency in Action

It's time to use the first/then contingency in a few examples so you can apply it to your unique home or classroom situations.

FIRST/THEN CONTINGENCY IN THE HOME

Do you seek to improve the behavior of loved ones who struggle with attention, focus, or large tasks? Then, you'll need a first/then contingency with smaller, more manageable tasks. Some learners have trouble with detailed tasks; others find some tasks extremely aversive. As a result, they can forget about the more appealing "then" promise, especially if the "first" activity takes a long time.

If an action takes a long time or has multiple parts, break it into smaller steps. Each portion of the task should have its own first/then contingency. This clarification helps them understand the process and gives them more immediate access to preferred outcomes. Consider these requests:

- "First, come and sit with your hands on your lap; then, Mommy will hold you."
- "First, brush your teeth; then, we can sit and read a book."

Your child may be neutral or even averse to sitting when you tell them to, and many children are averse to brushing their teeth. However, you know what will motivate your child. Play with the "then" portion until you find something that provides enough motivation to do the "first" activity without hesitation, whining, crying, or demonstrating some other undesired behavior.

- "First, put your laundry away; then, you can have time on your phone."
- "First, finish your homework; then, you can go to your friend's game."

Do you want your teenager to engage in an aversive chore? In a perfect world, they'd just do it. And you're working toward that. But, in the meantime, offer them a compelling reason to do what you ask. Encourage that preferred behavior with a first/then contingency.

Set clear expectations and provide a tangible, immediate benefit for meeting them. Think of it as a motivational bridge that helps your teenager cross from reluctance to action. With consistent application, this method promotes the completion of tasks while fostering a sense of responsibility.

FIRST/THEN CONTINGENCY IN THE CLASSROOM

First/then contingencies work as well in the classroom as at home! Here are some applications for younger and older school-aged children:

- "First, put your shoes on; then, you and your friends can play with Play-Doh."
- "First, walk inside from recess quietly with your hands down; then, you can have some free time to color."

A task may be difficult for children with motor skill challenges (a student may be slower to put on their coat, for instance). Perhaps the request just feels aversive (the student doesn't want to stop playing, or they don't want to have to sit down). In cases like these, students will be far more willing to comply when they know that a preferred reward is coming next. Here are a couple of examples:

- "First, I need everyone to remain quiet without talking throughout the test. Then, everyone can leave class early."
- "First, everybody should complete answers 1 through 10. Then, you can put on your headphones or earbuds and find some music on Spotify that you want to listen to."

The test or set of questions may take longer to complete, but with practice, students will develop greater self-control. They will learn to tackle the longer "first" tasks, knowing the "then" rewards are coming.

If the "first" task is highly aversive, make sure the "then" choice is particularly desirable. For example, don't offer pretzels or Skittles if a student isn't interested in those options. The reward must be worth the cost.

First/then contingencies help learners understand that "hard" or "boring" things don't last forever. With time, your loved one or learners will complete aversive tasks more often and more readily. Eventually, you won't need those preferred outcomes to see the behavior you want to see; your loved ones will begin to mature.

Back in Brightville, Alex learned to navigate challenging transitions, opening a world of possibilities for him. He enthusiastically embraced new activities, knowing he would experience something enjoyable after completing a task.

First/then contingencies promote desired behavior, ease transitions, and increase engagement in less-preferred activities for learners like Alex. By presenting tasks in a "first/then" sequence, parents and educators create a sense of structure that helps loved ones understand what comes next. As a result, transitions become smoother and more enjoyable for everyone.

APPLICATION EXERCISE

First/Then Contingency

INSTRUCTIONS

1. Think of a typical daily routine or a transition that your child finds challenging (e.g., getting ready for school, preparing for bedtime, leaving the playground).

2. Identify two steps for the transition. The first step is the current activity, and the second step is the preferred or desired activity that your child enjoys.

First:

Then:

3. Create a simple visual schedule using paper, sticky notes, or a digital tool. Write "First" and "Then" on separate cards or sections.

4. Write the first step on the "First" card/section (e.g., "Finish breakfast" or "Put on pajamas").

5. On the "Then" card/section, write the preferred activity that the child will enjoy once they complete the first step (e.g., "Play with a favorite toy" or "Read a bedtime story together").

6. Show the visual schedule to your child when the transition is about to take place. (Note: Providing additional "heads-up time" with reminders may be beneficial.) Use clear and simple language to explain the steps: "First, we will [first step], and then, we get to [preferred activity]."

7. Encourage completion of the first step by offering gentle reminders and praising your child for effort. Celebrate the achievement once they accomplish the first step and provide the "then" contingency.

8. Repeat this exercise for other transitions throughout the day. Observe how the first/then contingency helps your child navigate transitions and engage in less-preferred tasks more readily.

Consistency is vital to the success of the first/then contingency. Practice this technique regularly and adjust the preferred activities. Pay attention to your loved one's interests to keep them engaged and motivated. Enjoy the encouraging changes and smoother transitions that the first/then contingency can bring into your daily life.

BONUS VISUAL EXAMPLE

Don't forget the power of visuals! Visuals pair perfectly with first/then contingencies, and you'll read more about them later. It's nice if you don't have to constantly remind your loved one to do what you need them to do. If you want your child to do their chores before watching TV, consider creating a simple visual like the one below to help reinforce the correct order of events.

FIRST

THEN

To sign up for weekly tips from Bailey, visit us at:
BaileyPayne.com/Breakthrough

As adults, we do plenty of things we don't enjoy. It's inevitable. But those tasks seem more manageable when we have some choice or control over how they're done. Well, it's the same for your loved ones and learners!

BEHAVIORAL SKILL 5

Directed Choices

rightville was home to many spirited townspeople. And none were livelier than young Emma Reis. Emma was curious and adventurous, but her strong-willed nature often led to conflicts with her parents, especially during mealtimes.

Mr. and Mrs. Reis wanted Emma to eat a balanced diet, but she often resisted trying new foods and insisted on munching on her favorite snacks instead. So, they sought guidance from Mrs. Emerson, who had already introduced them to the first four behavioral techniques. Now, she was ready to tell them about "directed choices."

Mrs. Emerson explained that directed choices gave Emma a sense of control and ownership over her decisions while still guiding her toward healthy choices. The technique empowered Emma to make decisions within certain boundaries, ensuring that the choices were acceptable to her parents.

Emma's parents put directed choices into practice during dinner that first evening. Instead of telling

Emma what to eat, they presented her with two options for the main course: "Would you like pasta with tomato sauce or a grilled chicken sandwich for dinner?"

Emma had been prepared to resist the dinner menu but paused instead. "So I can choose what I want?" she thought. She considered the options and said, "I want the grilled chicken sandwich, please!"

Mrs. Emerson had advised Mr. and Mrs. Reis to offer praise and reinforcement for her decision-making. So, they replied, "Great job, Emma! You made a healthy choice for dinner!" They also knew to deliver her a preferred outcome for making such a healthy choice; they promised a preferred snack after she ate her healthy meal.

As the days passed, the power of directed choices (combined with other behavioral skills) transformed mealtimes for the Reis family. Emma felt more involved and empowered in her food decisions. She started trying new foods because she knew she had the freedom to make choices.

Emma blossomed into a more confident and open-minded child. Her newfound independence and willingness to explore different foods brought her parents joy. They were grateful to Mrs. Emerson for introducing them to such helpful behavioral strategies. Directed choices not only improved Emma's eating habits but also strengthened the bond between Emma and her parents, fostering an atmosphere of trust and cooperation.

Ask anyone if they'd prefer to have options in life or sit back and let someone else make all the decisions. Most everyone would shout, "Options, please!" Who doesn't love choices? We will harness that fact as we venture into the next behavioral skill, "directed choices."

ESSENTIALS
The Basics of Directed Choices

Directed choices are simple—they are options! But not just *any* options. These options are carefully curated by the people in charge and make sense in specific situations. Directed choices also encourage people to complete tasks and change certain behaviors. In addition to rewarding compliance, they empower people and demonstrate respect. As a result, attitudes tend to improve.

DIRECTED CHOICES

Options offered to guide loved ones and learners toward desired behavior or participation while providing a sense of control and autonomy within the set boundaries. These choices are designed to align with specific goals and tasks, ensuring that they support and encourage cooperation and desired responses.

It's essential to focus on the ultimate goal with directed choices. That goal is to guide others towards specific behaviors, like following a bedtime routine by brushing their teeth properly or completing their homework without complaining. These are the outcomes you want to achieve.

> **But here's the trick with directed choices: You offer some control in areas that are not particularly important.**

For instance, you might not care which room homework gets done in or which toothpaste flavor someone uses. Giving the child a say in these less critical decisions makes the overall task less unpleasant, reducing their chances of resisting or acting out. *The end goal is appropriate participation. Who cares about those little details?* You just want the child to complete the task correctly and with the right attitude.

Let's say a child is enjoying some free time on their tablet, and it's time to wrap it up. You can use a directed choice by saying:

> "You have fifteen minutes left on your iPad for the day. Would you prefer to use the rest of your time now or save the minutes until after dinner?"

This choice gives them some control over the situation and eases the transition from a highly preferred activity to the next task.

The skill is especially effective if the upcoming activities are aversive. Rather than dealing with challenging behavior, you can use directed choices to allow the child to voice a preference. Focus on the goal, whether it is homework completion, math class participation, or healthier eating. The goal is what matters.

A key to directed choices is to keep the options fresh and relevant. It won't have the desired impact if you offer the same choices every time for aversive or challenging tasks. You must mix it up and tailor the choices to the child's preferences.

For example, if reading on the floor isn't someone's thing, or you don't have cozy floor accessories like pillows and blankets to make the experience more appealing, then suggesting that as a choice won't work well.

Similarly, if you consistently offer a choice between a blue or pink pencil for math homework, but the color of the pencil isn't a motivating factor for the learner, it won't be effective. Instead, consider offering choices like using a marker or a highlighter. If your child enjoys markers and those are not always readily available, the option is more meaningful and motivating.

Keep the choices diverse and desirable each time you present them. That way, you'll increase the chances of your options having the desired impact.

REASONING
Why Directed Choices Work

When you push someone into an activity they find challenging or unpleasant without giving them any say, you make the situation more difficult.

Instead, let the child choose something related to the task or activity. This decision-making power makes them feel more in control, and when people feel that way, they're more likely to cooperate and respond favorably to what you're asking.

> Directed choices give loved ones and learners "buy-in." They feel like an essential part of the process rather than unimportant participants under the control of someone else.

As an adult, you want to be seen, heard, and valued. When you have the freedom to make choices throughout the workday, you feel more satisfied with your work. No one likes to be micromanaged. It's the same with children. When you ask them to participate in an activity they don't particularly like, allow them to choose something they *do* like. Choice, freedom, and a sense of control boost their satisfaction, resulting in more prosocial behavior and a decrease in challenging behavior.

APPLICATION
Directed Choices in Action

Practicing directed choices is quick and easy. Here are the steps to implement this strategy at home, in the community, or in the classroom:

1. **Identify the situation.** Begin by recognizing situations where directed choices can be beneficial. These are typically moments when you anticipate resistance, transitions between activities, or tasks that your loved one or learner may find challenging.

2. **Offer genuine choices.** Provide authentic and meaningful choices. These options should encourage a desired behavior or outcome. Avoid presenting choices that don't matter at all, as this could lead to confusion or frustration (and even feel insulting).

3. **Respect decisions.** Once you offer the choices, respect the child's decision, no matter which option they select. Doing so demonstrates care and lets them know that you value their choices.

4. **Provide praise.** When your loved one or learner makes a choice that aligns with the desired behavior or transition, offer praise and reinforcement. Feedback reinforces the connection between their choices and outcomes, encouraging them to continue making better decisions.

5. **Be consistent.** Consistency is vital to the success of directed choices. Implement this strategy regularly in your interactions. Doing so establishes a routine that encourages trust, cooperation, autonomy, and confidence.

It's important to note that if your loved one or learner rejects the choices you offer, you should not always offer new choices. Sometimes, you need to stick with your initial options; you can offer additional choices at other times. You want the child to have a sense of control in aversive situations, but be careful not to reinforce denials and avoidance.

DIRECTED CHOICES IN THE HOME

It's time to use directed choices in a few examples so you can apply them to your home life. Let's say it's time to transition to the bedtime routine. You might say:

- "It's time to brush our teeth. Do you want Mommy to brush her teeth with you, or do you want to brush your teeth by yourself?"

- "Alright, it's almost bedtime! Do you want to brush your teeth before or after we read your favorite bedtime story?"

You offer a choice that ensures the child will brush their teeth (a necessary task) but gives them control over the order of activities.

Here's another example to help a child transition from the park to the car:

- "Okay, playtime at the park is over. Would you like to hop into the car now and choose the music we listen to on the way home, or would you prefer one last round on the swings before we head back?"

In this situation, you offer a choice that ensures your child will leave the park, but it allows them to have some control over the transition by deciding whether to go straight to the car or enjoy one final swing. This approach can make the transition smoother and reduce resistance or tantrums.

Here are some other choices you can use in the home:

- "You can choose between your blue shirt and your red one. Which one do you want to wear today?"
- "It's time to put away your toys. Would you like to start with the dolls or the cars?"
- "You can watch one episode of your favorite show or have thirty minutes of video game time. Which one would you prefer?"

These options allow your child to make simple decisions and transition more smoothly between activities at home. It helps them feel a sense of control and independence while keeping the routines structured and manageable.

Now, let's say your teen hates homework time. Here are some suggestions to help make that transition a little smoother:

- "Would you like to complete your homework on the porch or sitting on the trampoline?"
- "After thirty minutes of work, you can have a ten-minute break. Would you like to take your break outside or inside the house?"
- "Do you want me to check in with you in thirty minutes to see how it's going, or would you prefer to let me know when you're done?"
- "Once you finish your homework, you can choose a twenty-minute activity you enjoy. What would you like to do as your reward?"

Remember, the key is to provide choices relevant to the homework process and allow your teen some control. Be sure to respect their choice. Use this skill to empower your teen to take ownership of their work and reduce resistance.

DIRECTED CHOICES IN THE CLASSROOM

Directed choices in the classroom can work wonders for educators! Let's say your students have trouble transitioning to reading time, which can be an aversive activity for learners with reading skill deficits. To help ease the transition, you might tell the learner:

- "It's time to transition to reading. Would you like to sit on the bouncy ball while you read or would you like to lie down to read?"

Another example is PE class, which might be unpleasant to certain students (e.g., the class might contribute to their sensory overload). You can make the matter less aversive by delivering choice and control.

- "It's time for PE. Would you like to participate in basketball today, or would you like to stretch on the sidelines?"

Both options involve physical activity, which is the end goal. But in some cases, you must be willing to pick your battles by delivering choice in what physical activity the student chooses.

Older students need choices, too! Here are some directed choices you can use with older youth and teens within a classroom setting:

- "Today, you can choose whether to start with the reading assignment or the writing task. Which one would you like to tackle first?"
- "During independent study time, you can work in the library or in a designated classroom area. Where would you like to work today?"
- "When you present your project, you can use slides or give a traditional speech. How would you like to present your findings?"
- "For the test review, you can work independently using a study guide or collaborate with a study partner. Which approach do you prefer?"

These options give students a say in their learning process and encourage a sense of ownership and responsibility. Directed choices can enhance engagement and motivation while respecting their preferences and learning styles.

When Mrs. Emerson introduced Emma's parents to directed choices, they learned that offering choices can be a powerful tool to guide behavior and foster cooperation. They found that options can give a sense of control, even in the simplest decisions, turning transitions and challenges into opportunities for growth.

Like the residents of Brightville, we can apply this behavioral skill to encourage prosocial behavior, reinforce autonomy, and nurture a sense of community where everyone can thrive.

APPLICATION EXERCISE

Directed Choices

INSTRUCTIONS

It's time to put your knowledge of directed choices into practice. Create two sets of directed choices—one for cleaning the room and one for setting the table for dinner—following the steps from the chapter. Feel free to tailor these choices to your child's preferences.

Once you've created these directed choices, you'll be better prepared to implement them to promote cooperation and prosocial behavior.

1. **Identify the situation(s):**
   - Cleaning their room
   - Setting the table for dinner

2. **Offer genuine choices:** Think about the choices you can offer related to each task. Make sure that the options are authentic and meaningful.

Directed choices for cleaning their room:

Directed choices for setting the table for dinner:

3. **Respect decisions:** Respect your child's decisions for each task.

4. **Provide praise:** Reinforce prosocial choices with praise and feedback.

5. **Be consistent:** Use directed choices regularly to establish a routine and encourage cooperation.

As a bonus, here is your chance to develop more ways to use directed choices. In the table below, identify three activities or routines that often present a challenge in your day. Next, note what portions of that routine are ideal times to offer choices and give up a little control. Finally, write down two desired choices that you could offer for that situation.

AVERSIVE ROUTINE OR ACTIVITY	PORTIONS OF THE ROUTINE WHERE I CAN OFFER CHOICE	DIRECTED CHOICES EXAMPLES
		1. 2.
		1. 2.
		1. 2.

A firm "no" can be a loving response when it helps our loved ones make better choices.

BEHAVIORAL SKILL 6

Addressing Denials

Laughter was once again filling the homes of Brightville. But in the home of the Chengs, laughter seemed to be in short supply. Eric Cheng was struggling to accept "no" as an answer. His mom was determined to help Eric understand boundaries and make better choices, which is why Mrs. Emerson introduced Mrs. Cheng to a powerful technique called "addressing denials."

Mrs. Emerson sat down with Eric and his mother to explain the concept. Addressing denials involved respectfully saying "no" or denying a request to the child, then immediately offering an equally appealing alternative. It was important to communicate when that desired request would be available.

To illustrate, Mrs. Emerson asked Eric if he was allowed to have chocolate or candy before dinner. He frowned and replied, "No. My mom never lets me," as he folded his arms.

With a warm tone, Mrs. Emerson said, "I understand why you'd want chocolate before dinner, Eric, but those are the kinds of treats to eat after dinner. The next time you ask for chocolate, what if your mom offers you fruit or a small snack bar instead? You could have chocolate as a treat for finishing your veggies at dinner!"

Mrs. Emerson encouraged Eric's mom to apply the technique at home consistently. When Eric asked for a sugary drink before bedtime, his mother responded, "We can't have juice before bed, Eric. But you can choose between a cup of milk or a cold glass of water. Then, at lunch tomorrow, you can have that juice!"

Eric felt involved in decision-making, appreciating his autonomy in selecting alternatives. Eric's resistance to "no" began to fade, and he gradually embraced the alternative options.

Parents and educators throughout town found this technique effective because it empowered their loved ones and made them feel respected and valued. By providing immediate alternatives within a context of love and understanding, caregivers saw denials transform into opportunities for improved decision-making. They inspired the young dreamers of Brightville to navigate life's boundaries with a joyful spirit and an open heart.

As adults, we're used to hearing "no." We've heard "no" since childhood, but even then, a "no" still stings sometimes. It's understandable, then, that younger adults and children with fewer coping skills may resent "no" and respond in an undesired way.

Saying "yes" is often easier, right? We're tired!

Well, I'm here to say that "no" is not a bad word. In fact, it is a *necessity*. You may think this assertion contradicts what you learned about stating things positively, but it doesn't.

Let me clarify:

When you state things positively, you provide a clear path to follow. But you can't say "yes" to every request, nor should you. Loved ones and learners *need* to hear "no" when a request is not correct, well-timed, or healthy. But what's important is *how* you say it and what comes *next*. If you never expose your children or students to the word "no," you fail to prepare them for real life adequately. So, let's get into it!

ESSENTIALS
The Basics of Addressing Denials

Nobody likes to be told "no." When you say "no" to something that your child highly desires, your denial can evoke a negative emotional response or challenging behavior. Let's say you're standing in the grocery aisle, and your child asks for a Snickers bar. You know that if you say "no," a tantrum or undesired behavior comes next. So, what should you do?

You can still stand your ground and deny the request. But don't just leave it at "no." Address the denial!

ADDRESSING DENIALS

The process of denying or saying "no" to a request respectfully, then immediately offering two available alternatives and letting the child know when the request will be available

As a technique, addressing denials has three steps:

Step 1: Just say no.

When a child asks for something unavailable, unhealthy, unproductive, or disruptive, tell them "no." I've heard professionals tell parents that "no" is a trigger word and to avoid it. So, parents and educators learn to dance around the word, trying to find a way to say "no" without saying "no." That practice needs to end. To be as successful and independent as young adults, children must learn to respond appropriately when they encounter words and phrases like "no," "wait," and "not right now."

Young people must learn to tolerate denial words without displaying challenging behaviors.

If we don't teach children how to accept denials, we're doing them a disservice. We've all had experiences with children and even adults who don't know how to respond correctly when they hear "no." As a result, they have meltdowns whenever they can't get their way.

We must stop sending people into the world who cannot hear "no" without a meltdown.

Children learn patience and resilience when they encounter denials. In addition to saying "no," you can say, "not right now" or "not at this time." The key is to be consistent and respectful.

Step 2: Deliver two immediately available options equivalent or close in value to the original request.

If a child asks, "Can I have some jelly beans?" you will not get the response you desire if you come back with, "No, but you can have some broccoli or peas." Those choices are not equivalent. Instead, present two preferred options that are in the same category. You could offer grapes, lower-sugar sweets, or organic candy alternatives. Or, if you are trying to stop your child from requesting sugary treats, offer two non-sugar choices that are not readily available; the options should be items that your child has highly desired in the past.

For many children, screen time or access to technology is a highly preferred activity. If your child regularly asks for iPad time, then TV time is not a great alternative, mainly because it defeats the purpose of reduced screen time. The two options still should be close in *value* to iPad or TV time. For instance, my children love water play, so I often suggest sprinkler time when I deny screen time. The second option could be playing outside, which is another preferred activity.

Step 3: Tell your child when their requested item or activity will become available.

It's important to tell children when they may have the jelly beans or screen time that you promised. Without this third step, children get the sense that the thing they want may never be available, which could increase the displays of challenging or protesting behavior. Instead, answer the question before they even say it!

Here is how I present it: "No, we're not going to have screen time right now, but would you prefer to play outside in the sprinkler or have Mommy swing with you? Then you can have a little screen time while I make dinner."

The ultimate goals are to 1) lessen the frequency of requests for an activity or a choice that is not readily available and 2) decrease challenging behaviors that result from denying requests.

REASONING
Why Addressing Denials Works

Using this three-step process to address denials is most beneficial when there is a pattern of challenging protest behaviors present after hearing denials such as "no," "not right now," or "wait until later."

This technique is highly effective in stopping challenging behavior for several reasons:

1. Respectfully saying "no" sets clear boundaries and expectations, helping the child understand that you will not grant every request. This consistency creates a sense of structure and predictability. The key is consistency. When you say "no," you must be true to your word, deny access, and *never* make exceptions.

2. Providing two immediate alternatives empowers the child with a sense of control and involvement in decision-making. It gives them a degree of autonomy, reducing feelings of frustration and resistance.

3. Explaining when their preferred choice will be available helps the child learn patience and delayed gratification. It fosters a deeper understanding of time and allows them to accept the present circumstances more gracefully.

By combining these elements, the technique instills a sense of trust, understanding, and respect between parents or caregivers and the child, leading to more prosocial and cooperative behavior.

APPLICATION
Addressing Denials in Action

This three-step process to addressing denials can feel overwhelming because responding this way is unnatural when you must deliver a denial. But you won't be using it every time you need to say "no."

Sometimes, "no" is enough!

Use this three-step strategy *only* when denying access to the most valuable preferences (unhealthy snacks and screen time are two of the most common times when you need to say "no"). You know the choices your child or students want the most—those are the times to pull this technique from the toolbox. Here are some specific examples:

ADDRESSING DENIALS IN THE HOME

You may repeatedly hear the same snack questions at home. Children always want a snack before dinner, right? We know we don't want them filling up on sugar and empty calories, and if they do snack, there are better options like fresh fruit, veggies, and clean protein sources. Here is how to word your response if your child asks for a snack before dinner:

- **[Step 1]** "No, snacks are unavailable until after your meal."
- **[Step 2]** "However, if you can't wait, you could have some milk, or you can go ahead and have your fruit from dinner, which will be strawberries."

- **[Step 3]** "If you eat all your meat and half of your veggies at dinner, you can pick a special snack out of the snack cabinet after dinner."

Notice that I didn't offer a book or toy. The child wants something to eat, so the alternatives should closely match. Also, I didn't use screen time as an option to address this denial. Parents often overuse screen time to avoid protest behavior because of its high value. The problem is that when you do this, screen time increases, and quality time in the environment decreases. Moreover, you undermine your most important goals: teaching your child to accept "no" and building tolerance for less-preferred but necessary tasks.

I usually provide milk and fruit with dinner, so those two options will become available soon anyway, making them logical alternatives. I follow this process consistently, knowing it will significantly decrease the likelihood of outbursts and other challenging behaviors when I say "no" to a particular snack.

Let's say your child wants to drive to a friend's house. For whatever reason, you feel it's not a good idea at this time (you've never met their parents, it's a school night, your child has homework, it's getting late, etc.). When you denied this request in the past, it led to a big argument. What do you say?

- **[Step 1]** "No, you won't go over there tonight."
- **[Step 2]** "You can use my iPad to call your friend if you want a bigger screen, or you can have extra social media time this evening."
- **[Step 3]** "If you agree, you can go to your friend's house on Friday."

Both of these offers are in the realm of connecting with friends, so they are appropriate alternatives. You also establish when your child will be allowed to head to their friend's house.

ADDRESSING DENIALS IN THE CLASSROOM

It's circle time, and a child asks to get a toy out of their backpack. You know this will disrupt the class, but you also know this child will disrupt circle time after a straight denial. So, you say:

- **[Step 1]** "No, not right now. We're not going to get toys out of our backpacks."
- **[Step 2]** "But you may have this fidget spinner or this stress ball to squeeze gently."
- **[Step 3]** "After we finish circle time, you may have some free time and get the toy from your backpack."

You denied the request but gave two toy-related alternatives. The child also knows when their favorite will become available.

Let's say a high schooler asks to use the restroom, even though they just got the hall pass a few minutes before. You know from experience that this teen uses the bathroom as a reason to leave the classroom and meet up with friends. In protest, the student attempts to delay doing a less-preferred activity (the coursework). Here's how to address it:

- **[Step 1]** "No, not right now."
- **[Step 2]** "You can finish your math assignment to number ten, or I can help you move through the next few problems if you're stuck on a number."
- **[Step 3]** "And then you can go."

Assuming there is no real bathroom emergency, you have offered viable alternatives that give them an end in sight and may help them overcome the reason they are attempting to stall the work.

Addressing denials is a powerful tool to promote prosocial behavior and stop challenging behaviors, as we saw with Eric in Brightville. By setting clear boundaries while respecting a child's wishes, you empower them with a sense of control and autonomy, just like how Eric felt involved in decision-making with the alternatives presented to him.

The blend of respect, involvement, and patience nurtures a trusting relationship between parents, educators, and loved ones. Addressing denials can help pave the way to respectful communication! When they become respectful adults capable of hearing a denial, your loves ones and learners will thank you for teaching them to respond appropriately!

APPLICATION EXERCISE

Addressing Denials

INSTRUCTIONS

Consider a situation where your child or a student frequently displays challenging behavior after hearing "no" (e.g., having dessert before dinner, playing video games right before bedtime, or wanting to use a phone during class or study time).

Create a scenario for the exercise, presenting the denial and the two alternatives. For example, "Your child asks for dessert before dinner, but it's not an option." In this case, offer these alternatives: 1) have a piece of fruit now, or 2) get a scoop of nut butter (or nut butter alternative) to help take away hunger pangs.

Special note: It's okay for your child or student to decline any options and just wait for the next availability of their initial request. The most critical factor is holding firm on the initial denial.

Role-play the scenario with a partner (spouses, best friends, and teens are great for this!). Take turns being the child and the parent or caregiver. Practice delivering the denial gently but firmly, offering the two alternatives.

When it's your turn to play the child's role, choose from the alternatives and express your feelings about the decision. As the parent or caregiver, offer praise and appreciation for the child's decision-making.

Reflect on the experience and discuss how the technique made the child and the parent feel during the role-play. Explore the effectiveness of your denials in stopping challenging behavior and empowering the child to make prosocial, healthy choices. Take turns switching roles and creating scenarios to practice the technique with various problematic behaviors.

Once you implement the technique in real-life situations, observe how your child responds to the two alternatives. Notice their reaction when you explain when their preferred choice will be available. Continue using the technique consistently to reinforce prosocial behavior and foster a trusting relationship with your child.

Here is a table to help you get the most out of the exercise:

HIGHLY REQUESTED ITEMS OR ACTIVITIES THAT CREATE AN ESCALATION WHEN DENIED	TWO PREFERRED OPTIONS THAT CORRELATE TO THE REASON FOR THE REQUEST (E.G., FUN, HUNGER, THIRST, ATTENTION)	AVAILABILITY OF THE HIGHLY VALUED ITEM (E.G., AFTER DINNER, AFTER HOMEWORK COMPLETION, ETC.)	OTHER NOTES
1.	.		
	.		
2.	.		
	.		
3.	.		
	.		

Let's pave the way for our loved ones to rise to the occasion simply by telling them how they CAN rise to the occasion!

BEHAVIORAL SKILL 7

Antecedent Expectations

Brightville *was becoming* a brighter place once again. But more young people (and their caregivers and teachers) still needed help. One of those students was Ajay Reddy. Ajay had his quirks and challenges like any other child. He was also known for his boundless energy. In fact, his enthusiasm sometimes led to disruptions in the classroom, making it challenging for him, the class, and his teacher, Mr. Goodwin.

One morning, as the students gathered in the classroom, Mr. Goodwin noticed that Ajay seemed particularly fidgety and distracted. Sensing his restlessness, he decided to see if a new behavioral skill called "antecedent expectations" would help. Mrs. Emerson had told Mr. Goodwin that it was important to provide clear instructions and cues to help Ajay know what to do before each activity. Specific directions and signals help students like Ajay understand what's expected of them, making it easier to channel high energy into productive actions.

As the morning progressed, Mr. Goodwin began implementing this strategy. Before transitioning to different lessons and activities, he approached Ajay and shared clear expectations. He would say things like: "Ajay, as we start our math lesson, I need your eyes on your workbook with your pencil following along by writing answers," or "Ajay, during our reading time, let's remember to stay in our seats and raise our hands if we have something to share."

With clear guidance and a sense of structure, Ajay found it easier to engage in each task. He felt less overwhelmed by the transitions or unsure about what was expected of him. Instead, he enthusiastically embraced new activities, knowing how to participate and contribute in a prosocial way.

Ajay's story illustrates how clear instructions and cues can pave the way for smoother transitions and more prosocial behavior.

In our journey through Brightville, we've witnessed the remarkable impact of strategies that nurture desired behavior. Now, we focus on antecedent expectations—a simple yet profound technique that empowers those around us to shine. This strategy is about giving clear instructions to help loved ones and learners understand what's expected of them, reducing challenges, and fostering cooperation.

This chapter will explain how this behavioral skill works, describe its real-world applications, and show the difference it can make. Get ready to unlock the potential of antecedent expectations and transform everyday moments into opportunities for growth!

ESSENTIALS
The Basics of Antecedent Expectations

Remember your ABCs from earlier in this book? "ABC" stands for:

1. **A: Antecedent**—The event or situation that occurs immediately *before* a behavior. It includes the triggers or cues that may influence or precede a specific behavior.

2. **B: Behavior**—The observable and measurable action or response that an individual engages in. It is the focus of analysis in the ABC framework and the element we seek to change.

3. **C: Consequence**—The outcome or result that *follows* a behavior. Consequences can be positive (reinforcement) or negative (punishment), and they shape future behaviors.

This ABC framework helps us dissect and analyze behaviors by looking at what happens *before* (antecedent), *during* (behavior), and *after* (consequence) a specific action or event. For this technique, you will focus on just one of those elements—the antecedent or trigger occurring in the environment just *before* the target behavior occurs.

Remember, the target behavior is the desired or undesired behavior you wish to "target" for change. You either seek to target a desired behavior in order to see more of it in the future or you seek to target an undesired behavior to reduce its future frequency.

The good news is the antecedent is something you can manipulate! By controlling the "antecedent variables" in the environment, you can impact behavior.

ANTECEDENT EXPECTATIONS

The specific instructions, cues, or signals provided before a particular behavior or situation. These expectations help set clear guidelines for appropriate behavior in various situations, making it easier for the learner to understand what is required and reduce the likelihood of challenging behaviors.

In short, "antecedent expectations" are a way to proactively guide behavior by communicating clear instructions or rules beforehand. They are sometimes referred to as "precorrections."

However, the most important way to deliver effective antecedent expectations is to state the exact behaviors you WANT to see (which is often the direct opposite of how the child is currently behaving). Sometimes, it feels silly to be so specific, but if you want your child to rise to the occasion, you must be clear; otherwise, how will they ever get there?

For example, if a teacher asks students to "pay attention," that teacher is less likely to see the behavior they want. On the other hand, if a teacher says, "I want all eyes on the teacher, voices off, and pencils down," now the students know precisely what the teacher expects and how to comply.

Likewise, if a teacher tells a student to "calm down," they would be less likely to see the behavior they expect. But the teacher is far more likely to see the ideal behavior by being specific, like this: "Stand still, hands at your sides, voices off, then please choose a place to sit."

> **The phrases "pay attention" and "calm down" leave too much room for interpretation. They are too vague. In contrast, hyper-specific statements provide the precise guidance our loved ones and learners need to meet our expectations.**

Implementing antecedent expectations involves a straight-forward path to prepare loved ones and learners for appropriate behavior. Here are three simple steps:

1. **Identify the situation.** Recognize potentially challenging situations or triggers where it might be helpful to provide clear instructions, cues, or signals. These are typically moments when you want to redirect a child's behavior or set expectations. Evaluate these situations and identify areas where your loved one has previously struggled to meet expectations.

2. **Verbally define clear expectations.** Determine the specific behavior or actions you expect them to display in a given situation. Provide clear, concise, and age-appropriate instructions. In most cases, you will give verbal instructions, but for younger children, you can also use visual cues to clarify or reinforce your expectations. Use a calm tone when communicating. Most importantly, tell your loved one or learners what *to do* (the prosocial action) rather than focus on what you *don't* want to see (the undesired behavior). The clearer you describe the behaviors, the more likely you'll see compliance and follow-through.

3. **Practice and reinforce.** Practice the routine or behavior, emphasizing the specific expectations. When they follow the instructions correctly, provide descriptive praise and desired outcomes (remember those helpful behavioral skills?).

These steps can help you implement antecedent expectations effectively, encouraging appropriate behavior and reducing the likelihood of challenging behaviors after a trigger.

REASONING
Why Antecedent Expectations Work

Antecedent expectations (or precorrections) are a game changer at home and in the classroom. You risk unnecessary failure and adverse responses if you don't explain precisely what you expect before a child begins a task. And that will lead to a cycle of constantly dealing with their challenging behavior.

When you say things like, "Stop that" or "Don't do that," you only draw attention to their challenging behavior. Using those phrases also puts you on the "consequences" side of things, whereas antecedent expectations are PREVENTATIVE, occurring BEFORE the behavior. And here's the kicker:

Drawing attention to a challenging behavior can backfire, encouraging them to misbehave *more*. Certain children assume that some attention is better than none, even if the attention is negative.

Beware of "attention-motivated behaviors;" you don't want them. When a child does something you don't like, they may react with more undesired behavior to get another reaction from you. For these children, attention is attention. It doesn't matter if the attention is a reprimand or descriptive praise.

Try not to correct your loved ones or learners all the time, either.

For sensitive children, a steady stream of corrective feedback may feel threatening. If so, it may damage your relationship.

It's best to take a proactive approach that reminds them what to do (rather than what NOT to do). Clearly explain step-by-step what you want the child to do, then recognize their compliance with feedback that lets them know what they're doing right. You'll boost the chances of your child completing the task correctly. That means less *corrective* feedback and more opportunities to praise and reward the child when they meet your expectations.

In short, you'll have better control over a child's behavior at home or in the classroom. Plus, you will create a more prosocial environment where everyone thrives, and prosocial behavior becomes the norm.

APPLICATION
Antecedent Expectations in Action

It's time to explore ways you can use antecedent expectations. Here are a few examples. See how you could implement precorrections in your own environment.

ANTECEDENT EXPECTATIONS IN THE HOME

Diaper changes can often be challenging for many parents and caregivers, especially if they are working with a tired or fussy toddler. Here's how to use antecedent expectations to communicate your expectations clearly:

- "Lie quietly on the changing table and keep your hands and feet still. Then we'll sing 'Twinkle, Twinkle Little Star' together while I change your diaper."

By stating this antecedent expectation, you set the stage for a cooperative diaper change, making it a smoother and less challenging experience for you and your child.

During mealtimes, use precorrection to clarify expectations and prevent food-related challenges. Say something like this:

- "During mealtime, it's important that food stays on your plate. If you don't like something, it's okay to show it by shaking your hand or saying 'yucky.' You may also scoot the food to the edge of your plate."

You can use this strategy for older children and teens when you want to ensure productive conversations at home. The next time you'd like to connect with your teen, try this:

- "Can we chat for a few minutes? I'd like you to set your phone aside to minimize distractions. Let's both use a respectful tone, and then we can discuss anything you want."

Stating your expectations up front makes it easier for a teenager to engage in a meaningful conversation without unnecessary tension or distractions.

You can also use antecedent expectations to let an older child know how you expect their room to look after you ask them to straighten it. Say something like this:

- "Once you tell me you have cleaned your room, I will come look. I expect the pillows to be on your bed and all clothes hung in the closet. When I look under your bed, I should see totes of clothes only. All your dirty dishes will be downstairs in the sink."

ANTECEDENT EXPECTATIONS IN THE CLASSROOM

You can ensure orderly transitions when you leave the classroom and head into the lunchroom, recess, or other activities. Be sure to explain your expectations clearly. Try saying something like this:

- "As we walk down the hallway, please stay on the right side. Keep your hands down, use slow walking feet, and keep your voices off. It's important to respect each other's personal space by staying an arm's length away from the friend in front of you. I'll be watching for those who follow my instructions."

You can also use this technique to guide students smoothly between tasks in the classroom:

- "During our transition, I want to see everyone walking directly to their assigned spot on the carpet. Their hands should be at their sides. I'll be checking to see who does this successfully."

By clarifying your expectations, you create a structured environment that minimizes disruptions. You can even use this to help you in the winter before students go out to recess:

- "We want to stay warm outside, so let's put our coats on. First, slide one arm in, then the other. If you need help, raise your hand and say, 'Help.' Then, I'll zip up your coat. Remember to listen and use a quiet voice during this process."

These antecedent expectations help prevent struggles and make the task more manageable for young children.

For older students, clear expectations help promote social inclusion. Here's one example:

- "During lab today, let's partner with classmates you have never worked with before."

An antecedent expectation like this can encourage teens to broaden their social circles and foster a sense of belonging.

You can also use precorrections to clarify your expectations regarding the students' phones in the classroom. Try this:

- "During lectures, I expect everyone to keep their phones in their pockets or backpacks, out of sight."

These expectations create boundaries and promote focused engagement.

The most important aspect (and perhaps the most challenging) is reframing your language to be hyper-specific. Identify the precise behaviors you wish to see *before* students begin a task. Proactive instructions deflect negative responses and challenging behaviors before they start.

Lastly, vary your antecedent expectations. If you use the same precorrections before every routine, you can lull your students into complacency. Instead, make the most of the opportunity and encourage your students to memorize the rules. That way, you help them master the guidelines and increase their independence.

Just as it did for Ajay in his Brightville classroom, antecedent expectations provide a clear path to follow, reducing challenges and fostering cooperation. As we close this chapter, remember that setting clear expectations empowers your loved one or learners to navigate life's challenges confidently and harmoniously.

One final thought: If you repeatedly pair a routine with an antecedent expectation, be sure to test the clarity and effectiveness of your instructions. Remove the antecedent expectation and see if the child continues to demonstrate desired behaviors (which you have consistently and precisely prompted). If so, remove the antecedent expectation and move on to the next challenge. In this case, consider it a success. Well done!

APPLICATION EXERCISE

Antecedent Expectations

INSTRUCTIONS

Now that you've explored this strategy and witnessed its impact, it's time to put it into practice. This exercise will help you apply antecedent expectations effectively. Here's what to do:

Step 1: Identify a challenging situation.

Think about an ongoing situation in your home or classroom when a child fails to follow your instructions, challenges you, or displays negative behavior.

Step 2: Define clear expectations.
How could you set clear expectations regarding the child's behavior in this situation? What specific instructions, cues, or signals can you provide to direct the child's behavior so that it is more compliant and prosocial?

Step 3: Create your antecedent expectations.
Write down the expectations you've defined. Be clear, concise, and age-appropriate in your instructions.

Step 4: Practice and reinforce.

Now, apply the antecedent expectations to the situation. Patiently practice the strategy and remember to reinforce prosocial behavior with praise and feedback.

After trying this behavioral skill, take a moment to reflect. How did antecedent expectations affect the child's behavior in a challenging situation?

Use antecedent expectations consistently to establish an effective routine and encourage cooperation. Track your progress and make adjustments as needed. Share your experiences and insights here and with others, whether it's a parenting group, teacher, colleague, or friend.

Want to hear more from Bailey? Follow her on Facebook @baileypaynebcba and sign up for her emails by visiting:
BaileyPayne.com/Breakthrough

The saying "actions speak louder than words" is true, but the purpose behind the actions guides how we should respond.

BEHAVIORAL SKILL 8

Becoming Aware
of Behavioral Function

L̲ike every small town, Brightville had its good days and its bad days. The Park family faced more challenging days than expected because their son Jonah was a prankster. He had a heart of gold but often found himself in trouble because of his antics. Although Mr. and Mrs. Park loved Jonah dearly, they couldn't figure out how to help him change. They wanted him to be less impulsive and more responsible.

One warm afternoon, as they strolled through Brightville, the Parks ran across Mrs. Emerson. After hearing about Jonah's latest struggles, Mrs. Emerson sat down with the family and talked about behavioral functions. She explained that every action, no matter how puzzling, had a reason—a function.

"Jonah's behavior isn't just random mischief," Mrs. Emerson said. "There's a purpose behind it, a function he's trying to fulfill."

Mr. and Mrs. Park listened intently, eager to understand their son better. They learned that Jonah's pranks were his way of seeking attention. He craved their involvement in his life and the warmth of their affection.

This revelation was shocking to the Parks, but Mrs. Emerson explained that Jonah was seeking a different type of attention or more frequent attentional interactions. She also encouraged them not to blame themselves. Some young people, she said, have an exceptionally high need for attention, or they seek a different type of attention than their regular interactions.

Armed with this newfound knowledge, the Parks began to change their approach. Instead of scolding Jonah for his antics and expecting things to change, they started spending more time with him, engaging in activities he enjoyed. They praised his creativity and kindness, which made him feel valued and loved. The Parks also began to initiate some surprises and innocent pranks on Jonah when he needed a comical interaction. Most importantly, they became more aware of Jonah's undesired behavior and were extra cautious not to reinforce inappropriate behavior; instead, they waited for a more suitable time to give him the attention he sought.

Over the next few weeks, something remarkable happened. Jonah's behavior began to shift. His mischievous pranks became less frequent, replaced by a desire to connect with his parents more meaningfully. It was as if he had found a healthier way to fulfill his need for attention. Jonah also learned that his parents no longer reacted or reprimanded him when he made poor choices.

Brightville witnessed another powerful break-through, not by some enchantment but by the simple act of becoming aware of behavioral function. Mrs. Emerson's wisdom had once again worked wonders, proving that understanding the "why" behind the behavior is crucial. It can lead to significant growth in the hearts of children and adults alike.

As Jonah's story shows, this strategy works because it emphasizes understanding.

To successfully alter a child's behavior, you must first recognize its purpose. You must also focus on external factors and how they influence the behavior. Then, you can examine the outcomes and formulate a plan to modify the child's behavior.

What are your loved ones or learners receiving from their environment? What are they gaining from you and other sources that prompt them to behave in a particular way?

In other words, what's *really* promoting your child's desired and undesired behaviors?

Let's say you want someone to start or stop a certain action. First, you need to figure out *why* they are doing it (or not doing it). That's the behavior's function.

Understanding the motivation for a child's behavior helps you evaluate the circumstances that lead up to the behavior.

Once you have a good idea of what precipitated the behavior, you can start looking at what happened *afterward* (this part is just as important as the initial assessment). The reactions or results that follow a behavior tell you what keeps the behavior going.

ESSENTIALS
The Basics of Becoming Aware of Behavioral Function

In the simplest terms, "behavioral function" refers to understanding what someone gets from the demonstration of a specific behavior. It answers the question: "Why did they do that?" Becoming aware of behavioral function is about identifying what someone gets from their actions. It also reveals the driving force behind their action or inaction.

BEHAVIORAL FUNCTION

Why someone does a certain behavior—what they get or achieve from it. It's like figuring out why we do the things we do (or don't do).

Becoming aware of your child's behavioral function allows you to accurately address the situation and modify the environment with appropriate consequences. That way, you impact behaviors more effectively. It's like solving a puzzle by identifying the missing pieces. You can tailor your responses and interventions to meet the individual's unique needs and motivations, ultimately fostering constructive change and growth.

THERE ARE FOUR
FUNCTIONS OF BEHAVIOR

1. **ATTENTION.** Behaviors to gain attention from a social partner. Sometimes, people act a certain way because they want a social interaction or reaction.

2. **ESCAPE.** Behaviors to avoid something aversive, uncomfortable, or undesirable. Think about when you hit the "send to voicemail" option instead of answering a phone call to avoid a conversation you don't want to have.

3. **TANGIBLE.** Behaviors to access a tangible item or desired activity. Children might act a particular way because they want to play with a toy, watch a movie, or buy a new video game.

4. **SENSORY.** Behaviors that result in some type of sensory feedback or sensory sensation. It's all about experiencing the senses. Think about how something feels, like when you rub a soft blanket because it's cozy.

Understanding these functions can help you identify what factors in the environment are reinforcing a behavior. If you consistently respond to your child's behavior in a certain way, they will likely continue the behavior. In their mind, the response and the behavior are somehow related, as in:

"Whenever I do _____, my mom responds by _____."

It doesn't matter if the response is positive or negative; they connect their behavior to the response. If your child desires your attention more than anything, they will repeat behaviors that direct your attention to them.

Whatever the child's motivation may be, one thing is certain: consequences *always* correspond with the four functions of behavior listed above. To promote desired behavior, pay attention to your reaction when your child makes a better or more prosocial choice. Do you offer praise or a reward? Do you hug your child? Is your tone friendly? In these moments, your child will connect your positive attention to their desired behavior. Since they want the same results in the future, they will want to repeat the desired behavior.

By contrast, if you want to discourage an undesired behavior, change the way you respond. Remember, your child will connect the behavior to your reaction. You may be inadvertently reinforcing misbehavior simply by doling out certain consequences.

Arguably, the most common reason (function) children continue problematic or undesired behaviors is to avoid something aversive. For instance:

- Toddlers might throw tantrums to escape toilet training, which they find uncomfortable or boring.
- Preschoolers might act out at the dinner table to avoid sitting still for too long or to distance themselves from non-preferred foods.
- Young children might cry in the presence of new caregivers to escape unfamiliar faces or situations.
- Children may argue, walk away, or even toss their homework to avoid doing it.
- Youngsters might try to escape quiet, still environments like libraries or grandma's house by running outside.

- Teens may avoid family discussions or errands with their parents to escape social interactions or avoid discussing certain topics.

- Dishonesty can also be an escape mechanism to avoid punishments and other negative consequences (e.g., a teenager may lie about breaking curfew to avoid being grounded).

In these cases, behaviors serve as a way to avoid something unpleasant or uncomfortable. When dealing with escape-motivated behavior, you must provide an acceptable escape route or a delay to help the child cope with something they find aversive. For example:

Suppose a child wants to avoid doing their homework, so they procrastinate or misbehave. In that case, an effective intervention might involve planned breaks. By teaching your child to ask for an occasional break, you provide the temporary relief they seek while keeping them on track overall. Be sure to remind them that whining, outbursts, or other displays of undesired behavior do not work; they still have to do their homework, and in fact, misbehavior might even result in extra work.

In this instance, your intervention aligns well with their behavior's function—escape.

As noted earlier, another common reason (function) for challenging behavior is the desire for attention. It's important to remember that attention comes in various forms, including comments, eye contact, physical touch, facial expressions, or feedback (both corrective and praise). Here are some examples of attention-motivated behavior:

- A child may run away during a structured playtime and start a new game of chase. Or the child may hit a sibling or parent. In both instances, the child wants the parent or caregiver's immediate attention.

- Some children repeatedly ask questions about their favorite topics to engage in a conversation they enjoy.

- A child might complete a task and proudly ask for praise or feedback.

- Some teens seek attention by making jokes in class; they want to get laughs from peers. Others seek online interactions through social media; they want validation through "likes" and comments on their posts.

As you can see in these examples, individuals seek various forms of attention to fulfill their social needs. When dealing with attention-motivated behavior, your intervention should offer an alternate way of providing the desired attention. For example:

Let's say a student seeks attention by blurting out, which disrupts the class as a whole. You ask the student to raise their hand when they want to say something, and when they comply, you offer to give them time alone with an iPad. This type of reward is not an effective reinforcer because it doesn't correspond with the student's need for attention. If you want a more effective solution, pair the iPad time with quality interaction.

This intervention correctly aligns with the student's behavioral function: seeking attention.

Behavioral functions are established over time; they are patterns, not random occurrences. All behaviors serve some purpose in the person's mind (whether it's a purpose you are aware of or not). So, you must become mindful of the specific function of a behavior. That way, you can identify environmental factors that either reinforce or discourage certain behaviors. At the same time, you can address and deal appropriately with the underlying cause of a child's behavior (both desired and undesired).

REASONING
Why Becoming Aware
of Behavioral Function Works

Every action serves a purpose. If you want to change a child's behavior, your interventions must align with that behavior's function.

Think about it this way:

As an adult, your primary reason for going to work is to earn a paycheck (it certainly is for most of us). If your employer decides to replace your wages with stickers to reward your efforts, you probably won't keep going to work. Stickers are insufficient to motivate you to keep plugging away at a task. While you like the salary, you are also motivated by other factors, such as setting a good example for your children and contributing to society. Your employer may not motivate you to set a good example or contribute to society, but they can reward your work with a competitive salary. Stickers simply don't measure up. You need a reward that fits the task. In other words, you seek a reward that aligns with a "tangible" behavioral function.

Similarly, suppose a student exhibits disruptive behavior whenever they want to escape an unpleasant situation. So, you attempt to change their behavior. Every time the child demonstrates *desired* behavior, you reward them with a chance to pick a toy from the classroom treasure chest. The student loves the toys and may even tolerate something aversive now and then to earn a toy. However, in this instance, the child is really seeking an *escape*. The reward system you've chosen doesn't align with their need to avoid an unpleasant situation. Your intervention will not effectively alter the behavior unless you address the behavioral function.

Understanding the function of behavior is crucial if you hope to apply effective interventions. You must address the true cause of the child's behavior.

When you dive deeper into the science, you discover that behaviors are not arbitrary. Instead, they exist as a means of achieving specific outcomes. Sometimes, the goal is to obtain something desirable; at other times, the goal is to avoid something undesirable. A student may act out in class, not because they are inherently disruptive but to avoid a difficult task or to gain the attention of their peers.

As an adult, you might notice that a colleague consistently arrives late to meetings—not out of disrespect, but because they're struggling with personal issues, and those issues produce some escape-motivated behaviors that affect their punctuality. Likewise, it's important to look beneath a child's surface behaviors to the root causes.

If you merely reprimand a student without understanding the reasons behind their actions, your intervention could miss the mark or exacerbate the problem.

Additionally, there are often *multiple* functions behind a single behavior. For example, a teenager might participate in a team sport for 1) the benefits of physical health (to *escape* health problems down the road), 2) the joy of the activity (to access a preferred *tangible* activity), and 3) the social aspect of group workouts (to access *attention* and social interaction). As a result, you need a *comprehensive* understanding of the teen's behavioral functions if you want to motivate or alter their behavior effectively.

Combining empathy and analysis is vital if you hope to bring about meaningful change in a child's behavior. Your efforts to understand the child's behavior can result in successful interventions tailored to the individual's unique motivations and needs.

Only when you align your interventions with the functions of behavior can you hope to inspire lasting, beneficial change.

APPLICATION
Becoming Aware of Behavioral Function

Understanding the function of a behavior is key to developing strategies that genuinely meet needs. To identify a behavioral function, you can use an approach we discussed earlier in this book—collecting data through the three-term contingency: A (antecedent), B (behavior), and C (consequence).

After you have collected your ABC data, look for ways to modify the antecedent/environment to encourage prosocial behavior and achieve a desired outcome.

Remember, antecedents clue you into the triggers or motivation behind the behavior. They can help you alter an environment and prevent undesired behaviors. Then, look for recurring patterns—because those patterns will reveal the "why" (or function) of behaviors.

For example, you might notice that a child receives attention (the consequence) seven times out of ten when they misbehave. From that data, you can conclude that the misbehavior is attention-motivated 70 percent of the time. This insight should guide your intervention strategy. Address the behavioral function (in this case, the desire for more attention).

To chart the cause and effect of the behavior, log the antecedent, behavior, and consequence. It might look something like this:

TANGIBLE-MOTIVATED BEHAVIOR IN PUBLIC

ANTECEDENT	BEHAVIOR	CONSEQUENCE
Child enters grocery store with parent	Child screams, cries, and flails body while sitting in the shopping cart	Child receives a piece of candy
Child enters gas station with parent	Child cries and throws body onto the floor	Child receives a pack of gum
Child enters fast food restaurant for lunch with family	Child screams and cries while tugging at parent's arm	Child receives a hug, a treat from mom's purse, and a request to "quiet down"
Child enters mall with parent	Child screams, cries, and runs away from parent	Child receives a cookie

Analysis of Behavior Function: The child has learned that displaying tantrum-like behavior in public often results in receiving a preferred reward (tangible). When the child enters a public space, 75 percent of undesired behaviors are followed by receiving a tangible, edible treat.

Strategy: Tell the child *before* entering the place that they may ask nicely for candy or a treat. Use first/then contingencies to describe that shopping/other goal will be completed *first,* and *then* they may select a treat. Use descriptive praise for the desired behavior. Also praise the child for their tolerance when waiting for the treat. Maintain consistency with consequences; do not reward tantrum-like behavior with treats.

ESCAPE-MOTIVATED BEHAVIOR BEFORE HOMEWORK

ANTECEDENT	BEHAVIOR	CONSEQUENCE
Parent says it is time to do homework	Learner gives no response and continues watching TV	Parent continues washing dishes and starts talking to spouse
Parent says it is time to do homework	Learner walks away from parent to the bedroom and shuts door	Parent turns off the TV and sits at the kitchen table waiting for learner
Parent says it is time to do homework	Learner argues with parent and insists she is not doing homework until after dinner	Parent makes a plate of food for the learner
Parent says it is time to do homework	Learner provides no response and continues watching TV	Parent turns off the TV and waits for the learner to start homework

Analysis of Behavior Function: From the data collected, the learner displayed escape-motivated behavior 100 percent of the time when requested to transition to doing homework. In other words, the behavior serves as an escape mechanism from potentially challenging or undesired work.

Strategy: *Before* asking the learner to start working on homework (transitioning to the task), tell her that she may request breaks, ask for help, or divide the homework into smaller amounts and work on the sections a little at a time. Provide several antecedent warnings for "homework time" (offer ten-minute and five-minute warnings). Utilize first/then contingencies by telling the learner to do the first five problems and then take a ten-minute TV break. Use descriptive praise when the learner transitions appropriately to homework time. Maintain consistency with consequences; do not reward undesired behavior when the learner tries to escape or delay the work.

ESCAPE-MOTIVATED BEHAVIOR DURING RECESS

ANTECEDENT	BEHAVIOR	CONSEQUENCE
Class transitions out-side to recess	Student sits at the top of the slide alone	The other students avoid the slide
Teacher asks students to find a partner	Student looks at the ground, chews on his fingernail and begins digging in his desk	Student does not find someone to be his partner
A classmate asks the student to play a game with them	Student says, "No, I don't want to."	Student continues independent play at his desk
Classmates are talking about playing "Firemen Rescue" at recess	Student asks a class-mate if he can join and play with them at recess	The classmate laughs at the student

Analysis of Behavior Function: The data indicates that 75 per-cent of the time, the student's behavior is escape-motivated (desire to escape social interactions).

Strategy: First, the educator can adjust the antecedent by 1) orga-nizing group activities, 2) introducing a peer buddy system to make social engagement more accessible and less intimidating, and 3) incorporating a reinforcement system that encourages social inter-actions with friends the students don't usually play with. After one or more of these adjustments, give the student appropriate options if he feels uncomfortable. Have this conversation *before* you ask students to interact with peers. If he does not wish to engage, he may 1) say "no thanks," 2) interact for just a little bit, then take a break, or 3) ask for guidance on how to interact and play.

Additionally, you should use first/then contingencies: indicate that *first*, the class will work in groups, and *then* the student may take a break and work independently. Provide descriptive praise for interactions and cooperative play. Maintain consistency with consequences. Do not reward undesired social isolation behavior; instead, reinforce assertive communication to indicate a desire for independent work and play.

ATTENTION-MOTIVATED BEHAVIOR AT SCHOOL

ANTECEDENT	BEHAVIOR	CONSEQUENCE
Teacher says, "Get out a reading book for quiet time."	Student leaves her desk and walks up to teacher's desk and asks if the teacher will read with her	Teacher asks student to go back to her desk
Classroom transitions outside for recess	Student leaves her seat and sits next to where the teacher is standing	Teacher asks student what she wants to play during recess and prompts interaction with peers
Teacher delivers a math lesson	Student interrupts the teacher to share infor-mation about what her dad packed for lunch	Teacher shares that it sounds delicious but it's time to get back on task
Teacher asks the class to share what they did over the weekend	Student raises her hand	Teacher calls on another student

Analysis of Behavior Function: The data indicates that 75 percent of the time, the behavior is attention-seeking (student desires to interact/receive attention from the teacher).

Strategy: Remind the student that *before* learning time and quiet activities begin, she should raise her hand and wait to be called on before speaking. Also, remind the student that you will not always call on her. Use first/then contingencies: tell the student *first* to work quietly, and *then* during lunch, you will sit next to her and discuss her favorite things. Provide descriptive praise when the student participates in an academic activity and when she uses her quiet voice. Maintain consistency with consequences; do not reward undesired behavior with attention-based interactions.

SENSORY-MOTIVATED BEHAVIOR AT SCHOOL

ANTECEDENT	BEHAVIOR	CONSEQUENCE
Teacher asks students to put away their water bottles	Student hops with cup back to the storage shelf	Teacher asks the student to use walking feet
Teacher tells the class it's time to clean up from lunch	Student continues eating his pizza and bounces on seat	Student continues eating as classmates near the student stand up to throw away their trash
Students play outside at recess	Student jumps up and down on the basketball court	A basketball rolls into the student's feet and disrupts play
Teacher asks students to get their backpacks and line up at the door	Student gets his backpack and lines up at the door while skipping	Classmates join in with the student skipping

Analysis of Behavior Function: Sensory-motivated behaviors often occur across multiple antecedents and have multiple functions. Behaviors driven by this need for a sensory experience are unique in that they can also occur even when the loved one or learner is alone. In other words, the sensory-motivated behavior will continue whether or not the student receives attention or the environment changes (the child simply displays the behavior to feel a certain way).

Strategy: Tell the student that he must use walking feet when in the classroom since this is the safest option. Use the first/then contingency: explain to the student that *first,* everyone walks inside the building, and *then* students may jump in PE, at recess, during music, and at sensory breaks on the trampoline. Provide descriptive praise when the student uses walking feet and jumps only during appropriate times. Maintain consistency with consequences. Do not reward undesired sensory-seeking behavior; for instance, do not give the student extensive time to engage in his desired sensory motions.

The ABC strategies can help you apply your understanding of behavioral function. As a result, you can take a structured approach to various behaviors, analyze their source, and implement a plan to make the corrections.

Recognizing environmental consequence patterns and understanding underlying motivations are pivotal first steps.

> By understanding the function of Jonah's behaviors, Mr. and Mrs. Park and the Brightville teachers saw the root issues. They looked beyond Jonah's surface-level disruptions to the heart of his motivations. As a result, the Parks enjoyed more peace at home. This new understanding also prevented Jonah's teachers from taking his disruptive behaviors personally or becoming frustrated with him as a student.

By harnessing the power of the three-term ABC contingency, you gain a fuller understanding of behavior, triggers, and patterns. This knowledge equips you to create targeted interventions that resonate with a child's genuine needs, resulting in long-lasting, desired behavioral change. *Understanding* the intricacies of behavior functions leads to empathy, insight, and effective interventions.

APPLICATION EXERCISE

Becoming Aware of Behavioral Function

Now, you're ready to apply the ABC strategy and deepen your understanding of behavioral functions.

Note: Becoming fluent in this topic takes practice, especially since behavior is complex and not always black and white. So, please take plenty of time to work through this exercise.

INSTRUCTIONS

1. Observation Phase: Over the next week, select one to three behaviors you frequently observe and wish to change.

2. Recording the ABCs:
   - Antecedent: What consistently happens immediately before the behavior?
   - Behavior: Describe the observed behavior in detail.
   - Consequence: What consistently happens immediately after the behavior?

Create a chart or table to document your observations. Aim for at least five instances of this behavior. Remember, establishing a pattern of consequences is most helpful.

Example:

DATE/TIME	ANTECEDENT	BEHAVIOR	CONSEQUENCE
October 11, 3 pm	Teacher assigns math problems	Student looks out the window, plays with a pencil at the desk, and hums a song	Student is reprimanded

3. **Analyzing the Function:** After recording multiple instances, analyze the data:
   - What patterns do you notice?
   - Based on the consequences recorded, what do you infer is the behavior's function? (If there is more than one function, list them as well.)
   - Are any external factors influencing the behavior (time of day, specific individuals present, etc.)? The antecedents column will provide this information.

4. **Developing a Strategy:**
   - Based on the inferred function(s), brainstorm potential strategies to address the behavior individually and compassionately.
   - Decide on a specific approach or strategy you would like to try.

5. **Reflection (after implementing your strategy):**
   - How did the behavior change, if at all?
   - What did you learn from this exercise about the importance of understanding behavior function?
   - How might you use the ABC strategy to understand and address behaviors in other situations?

NOTE: Remember that behaviors can have multiple functions; sometimes, it might take several observations and interventions to understand clearly. This exercise is a starting point and can be repeated as needed with different behaviors or in other settings.

Share your insights and experiences in discussions within our private Facebook group, **Behavior Breakthrough Community.** Doing so reinforces the concepts and fosters a sense of belonging and shared learning.

Without reinforcement, a Behavior Breakthrough is not possible.

BEHAVIORAL SKILL 9

Reinforcement

*J**ust beyond Brightville's** bustling square lives Tessa. Her energy is boundless, and her laughter is infectious. However, Tessa has had moments where her fiery spirit would cause rifts, especially at home.

Tessa's stepdad, Mr. Lawson, was often at a loss on how to manage her outbursts. He had tried numerous approaches, from stern talks to timeouts to gentle persuasion, but nothing seemed to work.

One day, he visited Mrs. Emerson and told her of their struggle. "It sounds like you might benefit from understanding the power of reinforcement," she calmly suggested.

Mr. Lawson was intrigued. He was excited to learn behavioral skills that might help him guide his stepdaughter. Mrs. Emerson said that every behavior, even the challenging ones, stemmed from a reason or "function." He discovered that Tessa often acted out because she felt overshadowed by her siblings; she longed for more attention.

Equipped with this knowledge, Mr. Lawson embarked on a mission. He decided to reinforce her prosocial behaviors by offering quality time whenever she communicated calmly and tolerated shared attention with her siblings. That could be a special story session, a walk in the garden, or simply helping her stepdad with a chore. The idea was to make Tessa realize she didn't need to act out to be noticed.

The change was gradual but undeniable. The house, which once echoed with Tessa's loud protests, now resonated with more laughter. Feeling understood and valued, Tessa began channeling her fiery spirit into creative endeavors, painting beautiful murals and crafting her own tales.

One sunny afternoon, as she sat in the front yard with her siblings, a neighbor asked Mr. Lawson, "What changed? Tessa seems so much more at peace."

With a grateful smile, he replied, "I learned to see the reason behind the behavior and how a little reinforcement can make a world of difference."

You've already read plenty about the term "reinforcement" in this book. Now, we'll examine reinforcement as a behavioral skill to help you fully grasp what it means and why it's crucial when guiding behavior.

ESSENTIALS
The Basics of Reinforcement

Reinforcement isn't just a fancy term; it's a foundational concept that plays a pivotal role in shaping and modifying behavior. Think of it as a bridge between understanding a behavior and effectively impacting it. When applied correctly, reinforcement can transform challenges into opportunities for growth and connection.

> **REINFORCEMENT**
>
> A process that strengthens a specific behavior by introducing a stimulus or outcome that follows the behavior and increases the likelihood of the behavior occurring again

Reinforcement is so much more than just rewards or praise. It requires you to recognize and respond to underlying needs, fostering lasting changes and building more meaningful relationships.

In chapter two, we discussed the difference between rewards and reinforcement, but as a reminder, let's clarify both. Think of a *reward* as a bonus or a treat. It's like getting a gold star sticker on your homework or a pat on the back for a job well done. On the other hand, *reinforcement* is like giving someone a reason to *keep doing* a good thing.

The most notable difference between rewards and reinforcement is that an effective reinforcer has been proven through *data collection* to impact behavior. In other words, you deliver a reinforcer and subsequently see more of the desired behavior.

> **If you notice a prosocial behavior happening more often because of something you did or gave afterward, that's reinforcement.**

Now that you have a better idea of what a reinforcer is and what it can do, let's apply that to the functions of behavior. We talked about being functionally aware of behavior in the last chapter. As you learned, it's important to respond to behaviors based on function. Doing so will help you implement the most effective behavioral skills for long-lasting behavior change. So, let's break down reinforcement for the four functions of behavior.

1. The child wants to avoid something. (Escape-Driven Behavior)
Some actions happen because a child wants to get out of doing something they don't like. To help reduce the instances of misbehavior, you can provide reinforcers contingent upon the child's display of *prosocial* behavior that also allows them to access escape—but in an appropriate way. Here are some examples of effective reinforcers that speak to the escape-driven nature of that behavior:

- Give the child a short break.
- Adjust the task a child doesn't like to make it more manageable (e.g., shorten the workload, decrease

the difficulty, allow the child to use a search engine to define words).

- Jump in and help the child out (e.g., assisting with tidying up their messy room).
- Allow a delay before participating in the undesired task or activity.

2. The child wants your attention. (Attention-Driven Behavior)
Sometimes, all a child wants is a bit of your time and attention. Other times, a child craves specific interactions or reactions. To encourage more prosocial behaviors, you can offer to:

- Spend quality time chatting about the things the child loves.
- Set up a special lunch date, just the two of you.
- Read or watch a movie together.
- Do little things for the child, like sharing a laugh or offering a hug (little things can work wonders).

3. The child wants a specific item/activity.
(Tangible-Driven Behavior)
This one's pretty straightforward. If a child acts in a certain way because they want a specific item or treat, then getting that thing can be a powerful reinforcer. For example:

- If the child keeps misbehaving because they want more time on the iPad, you can use small amounts of controlled screen time as a reinforcement.
- If the child wants a certain toy, that toy can be your go-to reinforcer.
- You can also offer to give a paycheck or an allowance to older children and teens.

- Video games, computer time, and TV time are also great reinforcers.

4. It just feels good. (Sensory-Driven Behavior)

Some behaviors happen because the child thinks they feel nice. To guide these behaviors, try offering:

- Tools or toys that provide desired sensory feedback (e.g., let the child swing or listen to their favorite song).

- Fill bins with preferred interactive sensory items, such as rice, beans, sand, or water beads; add small toys or objects that serve as "hidden treasures." Play "Find the Treasure." Allow children to play games with other interactive elements; that way, the children can still have a sensory experience while practicing sharing, taking turns, and communicating.

- Back scratches, massages, tickles, joint compressions, or tight squeezes may be effective reinforcers for sensory-driven behavior.

You can find the best way to reinforce desired behavior by focusing on the driving forces *behind* a child's behavior. Remember, this list is just a starting point for brainstorming. Reinforcement should be individualized.

Understanding unique sensory needs and preferences allows for the creation of tailored reinforcement strategies. By observing and learning what sensory experiences they find most rewarding, you can effectively channel their behavior in a positive direction. This approach ensures that the reinforcement is not only effective but also enriching for overall development.

REASONING
Why Reinforcement Works

Why does any of this matter? Think of function-based reinforcement as matching the right motivator (or reinforcer) to the reasons why a child behaves a certain way. Imagine using ice cream to motivate someone who doesn't like sweets; it wouldn't work, right? Similarly, you need to understand what lies beneath the surface to impact behavior. You must offer the right kind of incentive to encourage real change. Reinforcement speeds up the process. Here's why:

Reinforcement makes a tough task less aversive. We've all faced tasks or chores we don't enjoy. It can be even more challenging for a child to see the bigger picture and how an unpleasant task could be good for them in the long run. You can make aversive tasks more appealing by pairing them with a reinforcer (like a break or extra minutes playing a video game). Over time, you can offer those reinforcers less frequently, especially as a child participates more willingly and agreeably in non-preferred tasks.

Eventually, the child might even find satisfaction in completing the task, which speaks to the ultimate goal: *fostering intrinsic motivation.*

Reinforcement (fading over time) bridges external motivation to internal motivation. Not everyone is driven by internal motivation, especially during the younger years. For adolescents, knowing there's an external reward at the end of a task can be the push they need to act correctly. This external motivator can bridge the gap until the child develops their own internal reasons to behave well. This shift will be firmly established when you fade the reinforcement completely and prosocial behavior persists.

Reinforcers match the function. It's essential to ensure that the reinforcer addresses the root cause of the behavior. Handing out a cookie as a reward for desired behavior without understanding why a child acts out will likely not lead to effective change. The cookie becomes a reward, not a reinforcement. You create a more profound, impactful change by addressing the underlying reason for the behavior.

You're reading this book to become a better parent, therapist, teacher, or simply a more understanding individual. The true reward, or reinforcement, will be seeing these strategies work in real life. As you begin to guide behavior in your home, classroom, or other environment, you'll realize how understanding the reasons behind a child's behavior can lead to powerful change.

APPLICATION
Reinforcement in Action

It's time to use reinforcements in a few examples so you can apply them to your unique home or classroom situations. To make this section more relevant, I've broken down the examples according to the four behavior functions:

1. Escape-Motivated Behavior
Behaviors motivated by the desire to avoid or escape tasks or aversive situations

HOME
- **Scenario:** Your child doesn't want to do their homework.
- **Reinforcement:** After completing half of it, they get a ten-minute break to play outside. Gradually increase

the work time before the breaks as they get more accustomed to the task.

CLASSROOM

- **Scenario:** A student consistently tries to leave during math lessons.
- **Reinforcement:** After completing a portion of the lesson, they get to be a "helper" for five minutes, assisting the teacher with a simple task. Over time, reduce the frequency of breaks as they become more engaged in the lesson.

Note: For more severe escape-motivated behaviors, it may be necessary to present a task, allow the learner to ask appropriately for a break, and then allow the student to have a break before participating in the task. This process will build transition tolerance.

2. Attention-Motivated Behavior
Behaviors aimed at getting social attention or interactions

HOME

- **Scenario:** Your child is shouting or causing disruptions when you're on a phone call.
- **Reinforcement:** Let them know before the call that if they can play quietly during your call, you'll spend fifteen minutes doing an activity of their choice once you are off the phone.

CLASSROOM

- **Scenario:** A student often calls out or interrupts the class.
- **Reinforcement:** Provide them a responsibility, such as being the "class question leader." Whenever they

want to answer or ask something, they use a signal (like raising a special card). If they use this system effectively, you can praise them in front of the class for their leadership (confirm they enjoy public praise or this will not have the desired effect).

3. Tangible Motivated Behavior

Behaviors driven by the desire to access specific items or activities

HOME

- **Scenario:** Your child keeps grabbing snacks before dinner.
- **Reinforcement:** Create a reward chart where they get to choose a special weekend treat or activity if they wait for snack times or eat their dinner first. They should demonstrate consistency throughout the week.

CLASSROOM:

- **Scenario:** A student often tries to access the computer or iPad without permission.
- **Reinforcement:** Set up a system where students earn "tech time tokens" for desired behavior or completed tasks. They can exchange these tokens for supervised periods on the device.

4. Sensory-Driven Behavior

Behaviors exhibited to get specific sensory feedback or stimulation

HOME

- **Scenario:** Your child frequently seeks sensory input by spinning or rocking.
- **Reinforcement:** Introduce a sensory corner with tools/toys that cater to this need, such as a swing or weighted blanket. They can access this corner after asking politely

or completing chores or tasks, or you can base it on a schedule they help create.

CLASSROOM

- **Scenario:** A student often disrupts lessons by tapping objects or making noises for sensory feedback.
- **Reinforcement:** Provide them with sensory tools like fidget spinners or putty that they can use quietly. They earn access to these tools by showing prosocial behavior in class.

In each scenario, the reinforcement is designed to manage the problematic behavior and guide the child toward more adaptive and constructive behaviors over time. The new behaviors are the ones you want to encourage and see more often.

Mr. Lawson, once baffled by Tessa's fiery outbursts, found that the key to harmony was not in quelling the flames but in channeling them with care and attention. Tessa's murals and stories now adorn their home, symbols of a newfound peace. The echoes of conflict have been replaced by the music of collaboration and mutual respect. In Brightville, a family learned that the heart of change lies in seeing beyond behavior to the vibrant spirit and unmet needs within.

The importance of tailoring your responses to the behavioral function cannot be overstated. As we close this chapter, let's carry forward the lessons from Brightville and the behavioral skills we discussed, ensuring that our interactions, whether as parents, educators, or friends, are always informed and impactful.

APPLICATION EXERCISE

Reinforcement

INSTRUCTIONS

In the table below, fill in your examples of reinforcers for each behavioral function. In the second column, you'll find more generalized suggestions. Take a few moments to develop specific ideas that fit your unique circumstances.

BEHAVIORAL FUNCTION	EXAMPLES OF REINFORCERS	YOUR REINFORCEMENT IDEAS
Attention-Motivated Behavior	1. Praise and verbal acknowledgment 2. One-on-one time (e.g., reading a book together) 3. Engaging in a preferred activity with the child	1. 2. 3.
Escape-Motivated Behavior	1. Short breaks from a task 2. Choice of task order (e.g., which part of homework to do first) 3. Offering assistance with a challenging task	1. 2. 3.

Tangible-Motivated Behavior	1. Access to a favorite toy or item 2. Special privileges (e.g., extra playtime) 3. Earning points toward a bigger reward	1. 2. 3.
Sensory-Motivated Behavior	1. Listening to calming or preferred music 2. Using sensory toys or tools (e.g., fidget spinners) 3. Time in a quiet or comfortable space	1. 2. 3.

Reflect on the behaviors you've observed in your loved ones or students. With a clearer understanding of their behavioral functions, consider how to use reinforcements to promote prosocial behaviors. Remember, reinforcement isn't just about reacting to behaviors; it's about *proactively* shaping and guiding behaviors in a better direction. The more you can align your reinforcers with the underlying sought-after consequence of the behavior, the more effective you'll be in fostering lasting change.

Visuals can remove the need for assistance and present complex instructions in doable steps.

BEHAVIORAL SKILL 10

Visuals

*I*n *Brightville,* where tales and teachings intertwine, there lived a gifted teacher named Mrs. Gentry. She was eager to bring out the best in her students, but despite her best efforts, she struggled with a student named Kian. He was bright and energetic but often found it challenging to follow instructions and focus on tasks. Mrs. Gentry tried different teaching methods, but nothing seemed to help Kian stay on track.

One afternoon, Mrs. Gentry met with Mrs. Emerson, who was known to have solutions for even the most challenging situations. As they exchanged pleasantries, the teacher hesitated momentarily before expressing her concerns about Kian. Mrs. Emerson listened intently, nodding now and then. When Mrs. Gentry finished, Mrs. Emerson said, "Have you ever tried using visuals? They can serve as a powerful link between expectations and execution."

The hopeful teacher's eyes twinkled with curiosity. "Visuals?" she inquired.

Mrs. Emerson elaborated, "Yes, visual aids, schedules, and cues. You can use these tools to guide Kian through his tasks, making them more understandable and less overwhelming. And most importantly, they will decrease his need for verbal prompts."

Inspired by Mrs. Emerson's suggestion, the Brightville teacher spent her evening crafting visual schedules for the next day's lessons. The classroom walls were soon filled with colorful charts depicting daily activities, group tasks, and behavior expectations. Some charts applied to the class as a whole, while others described her behavioral expectations for individual students. Mrs. Gentry put the individuals' charts on their desks.

When Kian walked into the classroom the following day, his eyes widened in surprise as Mrs. Gentry introduced him and the rest of the class to the world of visuals. For the math lesson, he saw a chart breaking down each step, from understanding the problem to finding the solution. For reading, a sequence of icons guided students from selecting a book to discussing its central themes.

The visuals served as a roadmap, helping Kian navigate tasks with newfound confidence. Whenever he felt lost, he'd refer to the charts, and he'd find his way. Kian's focus improved, his enthusiasm for learning was reignited, and he began to excel—not just academically but also in his interactions with classmates.

Kian could participate in classroom discussions more successfully and required less teacher assistance.

Grateful for the change that visuals brought into her classroom, Mrs. Gentry shared her success story with other teachers in Brightville. As days turned into weeks and weeks into months, the use of visuals spread across town, encouraging more Brightville townpeople, thanks to the wisdom of Mrs. Emerson.

The world around us is chock-full of visuals, signals that guide our every action and reaction. From the stop sign at the corner of a street to the glow of an exit sign in a dark theater, visuals are everywhere, influencing our behaviors without us even realizing it. This chapter teaches how visuals can transform a child's behavior without uttering a word.

ESSENTIALS
The Basics of Visuals

Visuals are powerful tools that help students with organization, scheduling, rules, directions, reminders, transitions, and reinforcements.

VISUALS

Any visual signal within an environment that prompts a specific behavioral response

Think of visuals as unspoken reminders. A visual can be as simple as a post-it note reminding a child to take out the trash or as specific as a photograph instructing them how to sit correctly. Moreover, these cues take many forms: environmental placements, notes, icons, or any stimulus that prompts a behavior change.

Visuals should convey a message without needing spoken words or prompting assistance. For example, imagine your child's lunchbox hanging on a peg by the front door. Its presence is a silent reminder that says, "Don't forget your lunch today!" Most importantly, the visual removes the need for a parent or other helper to remind the child to grab their lunchbox. That's the magic of visuals!

Visuals don't merely serve as reminders, decreasing forgetfulness. They also serve as environmental prompts for specific behaviors, increasing independence, desired behaviors, and self-awareness.

Visuals are incredibly versatile. They can be "singular," like a solitary icon or word, or "composite," like a list or a schedule with a series of actions.

What is the visual's primary purpose? To prompt desired behaviors and help loved ones and learners participate in tasks and display prosocial behaviors without requiring your constant prompting or attention.

Do real-world photos qualify as visuals or are they always cartoons or drawings? Using real-world pictures, especially those that feature the learner within their actual environment, often reduces the need for detailed explanations. The familiarity of real-world images makes comprehension almost instantaneous. Most learners eagerly pay attention to teaching materials that incorporate their own images.

Visuals, like photos or drawings, prompt the child to follow instructions with prosocial behavior, such as raising a hand or sitting quietly in the reading circle. They also reduce the need for adult intervention, boosting the child's independence. Once the child masters the rules, it's easy to "fade" the visuals.

Now, imagine a classroom. A teacher hangs a picture on her whiteboard showing a student sitting attentively. This photo serves as a guide for all students, signaling how they should be seated and focused. If any student fails to comply, a simple gesture toward the picture can bring them back in line without the teacher pausing her lesson or delivering quality attention for less-than-desirable behaviors.

You can also use visuals at home. Picture dinnertime: Your child is struggling to stay seated throughout the meal. You could place a visual of the table that shows them sitting and eating, using good manners. The visual reminds them to remain seated until you remove the image. No words. No fuss. Just a simple visual that prompts the behavior you want to see.

Words *can* serve as visuals, too. For literate learners, a word can be a powerful visual prompt. Think of a basket of toys with the word "SHARE" displayed prominently. The sign serves as a silent reminder that these are toys meant to be shared, potentially reducing squabbles.

Similarly, a simple "STOP" sign on a classroom door can instruct students to check in with the teacher before exiting. It's a silent yet effective way to manage behavior without constant verbal reminders.

In essence, visuals are silent partners in behavior management, fostering independence and reducing the need for ongoing direction. Indeed, they are indispensable tools to help shape behavior at home and school.

PRO TIP

Visuals are especially beneficial for visual learners who might find auditory information challenging.

Think of visuals like a roadmap, showing the way forward without much outside intervention. But how do they work, you ask? Here is a quick guide:

1. Single-Activity Visuals

Take, for instance, a child resisting the idea of cleaning their room. You can give the child a clear roadmap by breaking down the task into visual steps—a photo of Legos tidied up, trucks in a basket, books on a shelf, and a neat bed. The step-by-step format doesn't just tell them *what* to do; it shows them. This approach reduces overwhelming feelings and makes the task more approachable.

You can also apply this visual methodology in school. Let's say a teacher frequently deals with the students incorrectly completing their worksheets. Instead of giving them vague directions, the teacher can provide a visual sequence that *illustrates* the worksheet process: "Write your name. Read the instructions. Answer the first question. Ask for help as needed. Check your work after completion. Turn in your worksheet to the teacher." Whether it's icons, pictures, or written steps, this sequence encourages students to self-direct while fostering independence.

2. Multi-Activity Visuals

Imagine visuals as an extended playlist for your day. For a child, visuals could map out a morning routine, depicting activities from making the bed and eating breakfast to grabbing a backpack. These tools don't just promote task completion; they enhance organization and prosocial behavior overall.

Here's another practical example: Imagine a group of children on the playground, squabbling over the swings or arguing about who gets to play kickball. Rather than trying to control the chaos, the teacher could use visuals. Before leaving for recess, the teacher could point to the signs that show how to play nicely. The visuals could also suggest an order of activities (e.g., swings, kickball, then tag). In this instance, visuals guide the children towards constructive play and smooth playground interactions.

> **For visuals to be effective, it's vital to pair them with reinforcement—at least, initially.**

To explain why this is true, imagine two billboards (visuals) along an interstate.

- **Billboard #1 says:** "All drivers who refrain from cell phone use while driving will receive $100 at exit 110." This visual serves as a reinforcer because it is paired with money. The drivers will likely follow the instructions on billboard #1 because they want the reinforcement ($100 bill).

- **Billboard #2 says:** "Keep your eyes on the road." This visual may motivate drivers to keep their eyes on the road for a short while, but it likely won't improve their attention overall. The billboard contains no reinforcement, so the drivers' behavior won't change much.

When you pair a visual with reinforcement, the visual has more value. When the visual has value, learners feel more motivated to obey the visual.

Over time, as the task or steps become habits, you can scale back and eventually remove the reinforcement. The visual then becomes a self-sustaining tool that young ones rely on for guidance.

Eventually, you can remove the visual itself. If the prosocial behaviors remain and tasks are done correctly, you know the children are well on their way to independence and self-awareness.

PRO TIP

Be sure that visuals are displayed discreetly. If you're waving a visual in a child's face, you're doing it wrong. The visual should fit quietly into the environment, guiding rather than disrupting.

Visuals are stellar items in your behavioral toolkit because they make tasks less daunting and help students and children foster self-reliance. They are a game changer for behavior management in any environment where you seek improvement.

REASONING
Why Visuals Work

Understanding the "why" behind visual aids can be as important as using them. So, let's briefly discuss the underlying mechanics of their effectiveness.

1. Visuals decrease adult dependence.

The essence of visuals isn't some enchanting solution to behavior woes. Instead, they act as a buffer, minimizing the consistent need for adult intervention during challenging tasks. The fewer prompts from an adult, the fewer attention-seeking and unwanted behaviors you will see during less-preferred activities.

2. Visuals pair perfectly with reinforcements (that slowly fade).

Imagine a visual as a new employee and the reinforcement as their experienced mentor in the workplace. The reinforcer gives the visual a sense of credibility. "Look, my friend," the reinforcer says. "I will give you something good if you obey the visual!" *The reinforcement makes the visual more valuable to the learner.*

Indeed, this close-knit partnership between the visual and reinforcement is critical during the early stages of a task or activity. You should introduce a reinforcement whenever a child completes one task or moves from one step to another in a visual schedule.

Remember, visuals are not a forever fix. Their purpose is to *increase independence* while *decreasing the need for attentional interactions and assistance.* You want to enhance the child's self-awareness and encourage self-management skills. By slowly fading the reinforcement, you give the child time to adjust; they become more familiar with instructions and start to display independence.

Eventually, just like a trainee who becomes a pro at the job, the visual stands alone, effectively guiding the child.

> **NOTE:** If you remove a visual and the desired responses drastically *decrease*, try removing a portion of the visual or making it smaller. Then, fade the visual out more slowly or differently the next time.

3. Visuals help you evaluate your chosen reinforcement.

You should ensure that the reinforcement matches the child's preferences. That can determine the success of a visual schedule. If a visual isn't making the intended impact, the visual may not be at fault; it may be a problem with the reinforcement strategy. It's like having the best teacher in the world, but the learning will be stifled if the learner's needs aren't met.

If your visual is not making the impact you seek, here are a few questions:

- Are you offering the reinforcement frequently enough?
- Is your chosen reinforcement one that the child or learner genuinely prefers?
- Does the reinforcement correspond with the behavioral function you are targeting?
- Does the reinforcement match the behavioral challenge? (If the visual prompts the child to do something challenging, the reinforcement should provide enough of a reward to motivate the child to comply.)

When combined with thoughtful reinforcement, visuals can be powerful allies in fostering independence and prosocial behavior. They serve as subtle guides, reducing the need for external prompts and empowering individuals to navigate tasks autonomously.

PRO TIP

If your learner isn't responding to visuals, you haven't effectively paired the visual and desired behaviors with reinforcement.

APPLICATION
Visuals in Action

Visuals can make daily routines smoother and more efficient at home and school. They offer clear, nonverbal cues to help establish routines and expectations while encouraging independence. Here are some specific examples to consider:

VISUALS IN THE HOME

MORNING ROUTINES
Create a visual chart with icons representing each morning routine step. For example:
- Waking up
- Making the bed
- Brushing teeth
- Getting dressed
- Eating breakfast

CHORE CHARTS

Use visuals to depict common household chores. Charts can empower your loved ones to take the initiative without being told:

- Sweeping or vacuuming
- Feeding pets
- Watering plants
- Setting or clearing the table

BEHAVIOR EXPECTATIONS

Design a chart that illustrates acceptable and unacceptable behaviors, reinforcing desired actions:

- Sharing with siblings
- Saying "please" and "thank you"
- Keeping hands to oneself
- Limiting screen time

EXECUTIVE FUNCTIONING SKILL (TIME MANAGEMENT)

Visuals can help learners develop time management skills they need as they age. Here are some steps you could include in a visual to help children think about time:

- Evaluate how much time is available.
- Determine if there is enough time to complete the task.
- Start the task or select a task that can be completed in the available time.
- Check time throughout the process.
- Discontinue your participation in the task when you reach a certain time.
- Transition to the next activity in an appropriate way.

VISUALS IN THE CLASSROOM

CLASSROOM RULES
Visuals can remind students of basic classroom expectations:
- Raising a hand to speak
- Listening when others talk
- Staying in one's seat
- Respecting classmates' belongings

DAILY SCHEDULE
A visual timetable can guide students through the day's activities, helping them transition smoothly:
- Morning circle or assembly time
- Reading hour
- Math lessons
- Lunch break
- Art or physical education

GROUP ACTIVITIES
For group tasks or projects, visuals can clarify roles and responsibilities:
- Leader or presenter
- Note-taker
- Researcher
- Timekeeper

TASK COMPLETION
Break down complex assignments into manageable steps using visuals:
- Understanding the task
- Researching or brainstorming
- Drafting or practicing
- Revising or refining
- Final submission or performance

EXECUTIVE FUNCTIONING SKILL (COMPROMISING)

Visuals can help learners develop interpersonal skills they need as they age. Here are some steps you could include in a visual designed to help children think about the art of compromise:

- Evaluate what I want.
- Assess what the other person wants.
- Determine how we can both get a little bit of what we want.
- Offer the solution.
- Accept a smaller portion of what I want and respond appropriately.

Implementing these visual aids can pave the way for a structured environment where individuals can function with a higher degree of independence and clarity. As you begin crafting and implementing visual schedules, remember Kian in Brightville.

Mrs. Emerson's guidance inspired and enlightened Kian's teacher. Mrs. Gentry started using visuals to help Kian complete tasks without feeling overwhelmed. In the end, Kian was very grateful for this amazing tool!

Likewise, your efforts can illuminate the path for your loved ones or learners. With the right behavioral skills, used in the correct order, your story can have a happy ending like Kian's!

APPLICATION EXERCISE

Visuals

Objective: Develop visual schedules to address specific behaviors in your home or classroom that you find challenging.

INSTRUCTIONS

1. Identify problematic behaviors.

Jot down behaviors that you find challenging or problematic at home or in your classroom. These could be anything. Examples include a child's refusing to clean their room, getting distracted during reading time, bickering during recess, or needing a lot of prompting or assistance. Remember to be specific.

Here are a few other examples:

- **Screaming, crying, and running from homework**
- **Sitting quietly during group activities without engaging in conversation**
- **Arguing and whining during the transition from one activity to the next**

2. Choose a behavior for intervention.

Select one behavior from that list you want to address using a visual schedule.

3. Decide on the type of visual.

Determine whether you need a visual for a *single complex task* or a *multiple activity schedule.*

- **Single Task:** A behavior that revolves around one main task (e.g., cleaning a room)
- **Multiple Activity Schedule:** A sequence of activities or routines (e.g., a morning routine that includes several steps, such as getting dressed, eating breakfast, brushing teeth, checking backpack)

4. Break it down.

Deconstruct the task or routine into specific, manageable steps or activities. For example, if the task is emptying the dishwasher, you might list:

- Sort silverware into the drawer.
- Stack plates on the shelf.
- Stack bowls on the shelf.
- Place cups upside down on the shelf.
- Place serving utensils in the drawer.

5. Create your visual schedule.

Craft your visual schedule using the list you've made. You can draw it out, use printed images, or write down the steps.

If you're addressing classroom behaviors, consider using universally recognizable icons. Pictures from magazines or personal photographs can be highly effective for home behaviors.

Sequence the steps or activities correctly, and remember that you will need to teach the meaning of any symbols or cartoon images you use.

6. Implement and review.

Introduce the visual schedule to your child or learners. As they begin to use it, observe their interactions and responses. Adjust as necessary.

Remember the importance of pairing the visual with reinforcement, especially in the early stages.

7. Reflect.

After a week or two (once you have collected sufficient data to make an informed decision), review the results to determine the effectiveness of the visual. Here are a few questions you could ask:

- **Has the problematic behavior lessened?**
- **Is your child or learner showing more independence?**
- **If the visual has been successful, is it time to begin fading the reinforcer?**

Make notes on what's working and what might need tweaking.

Remember, the goal of this exercise is not simply to create a visual schedule but to enhance independence and desired behavior. Enjoy the process and celebrate the successes, no matter how small!

BONUS CONTENT EXAMPLE

Here are prompts for a visual designed to help your loved one or learners change their thought process if they are stuck on a particular attitude, outlook, or opinion.

**STEPS FOR GETTING "UNSTUCK"
AND CHANGING THOUGHTS**

1. Visualize a stop sign.
2. Think about something different.
3. Make a comment about something different.
4. Change environments and/or engage in physical movement.
5. Repeat as necessary.

Set a five-minute timer as you dive into this new skill. When the timer sounds, reward yourself with a snack, a positive affirmation, or some quiet time on your phone!

BEHAVIORAL SKILL 11

Timers

*I*n a quaint corner of Brightville, two siblings, Anya and Rehan, often found themselves in a tizzy during their daily routines. Mornings were a whirlwind, and evenings brought about the usual protest when it was time to transition from playtime to bedtime. Their parents, Mr. and Mrs. Kapoor, felt like they were continuously racing against the clock.

One day, Mrs. Kapoor saw Mrs. Emerson at the Brightville market. Seeing Mrs. Kapoor's distressed face, Mrs. Emerson inquired after her children. Upon hearing about the siblings' daily dilemmas, Mrs. Emerson offered, "Have you tried using timers?"

The next morning, Mr. Kapoor introduced a colorful timer, setting it for ten minutes. "Anya, Rehan, when this timer goes off, it's time to wrap up breakfast and get ready for school," he explained. "And if you're both ready before the timer rings, a surprise might be waiting!"

The timer's countdown created a sense of gentle urgency. Not wanting to miss their surprise, the siblings finished their breakfast quickly and got ready, beating the timer! Since they were ahead of schedule, Mr. Kapoor used the few extra minutes to let them play outside before loading up.

In the days that followed, the Kapoors incorporated the timer into various activities—setting it for fifteen minutes of reading time before bed and setting it as a five-minute warning before they needed to turn off the TV. Anya and Rehan began to expect and respect the timer's signals, seamlessly moving from one task to another. Instead of dreading transitions or reminders, they looked forward to them, associating the timer's chime with a sense of accomplishment and, sometimes, a fun little reinforcer.

The Kapoor family's success demonstrated how a simple tool, when used thoughtfully, can transform daily routines and reinforce desired behavior. And just like that, the little timer worked its wonders, bringing harmony to the Kapoor household.

As simple tools to measure minutes, timers come in various forms— from stopwatches to digital kitchen timers to applications on mobile devices. Their brilliance in behavior management lies in their neutrality. So, let's get into it!

ESSENTIALS
The Basics of Timers

Consider a typical scenario: your child is engrossed in a game on their iPad or entranced by a cartoon on TV. The end of their allowed screen time is drawing near, and as a parent or teacher, you dread the moment when you have to announce, "It's time to turn it off!"

Why? Because, more often than not, this interaction results in protest, frustration, or even tantrums. The child, who is thoroughly enjoying the activity, understandably finds it difficult to disengage. And when the signal to stop comes directly from you, it can unintentionally position you as the "bad guy." Your presence can even signal punishment.

That's where timers come into play. Instead of becoming the harbinger of disappointment every time a preferred activity has to end, you can let the timer take that role. This way, the end of an activity is no longer solely associated with you. It's the timer that signals the transition, not you.

TIMERS

Neutral environmental stimuli used to signal a cue or response, promoting independence in loved ones and learners and preserving positive associations with caregivers

---

The timer acts as a neutral party in the scenario I described. It's an inanimate object and not emotionally charged like a parent or teacher might be. Because of that, the child (frustrated by having to stop an activity) has to reevaluate their response. This allows their frustration to be directed toward the timer or the transition itself, not a parent or teacher.

Just like visuals must be paired with reinforcers, timers must be paired with reinforcement to be impactful.

When the timer sounds, it shouldn't just indicate the end of one fun thing. Instead, it should signal the request for a specific desired behavioral response. Children should learn that when they face transitions with a good attitude, it results in preferred outcomes.

Timers ease the child from one engaging activity to another, smoothing transitions and minimizing potential conflicts. By integrating this neutral tool into your routine, you cultivate an environment where transitions are less about loss and more about moving from one rewarding experience to another.

REASONING
Why Timers Work

Utilizing timers as a behavioral skill has many benefits. To understand their effectiveness, let's discuss the "why" behind them:

1. Timers promote self-monitoring and independence.

Imagine using a timer to remind a child to brush their teeth. By setting the timer and explaining the expectation (brushing teeth when the timer goes off), you give the child a sense of responsibility. They know the task, they're aware of the time limit, and they're in control of their actions.

As the child acknowledges the timer and completes the activity, they're not just brushing their teeth; they're learning to monitor and regulate their own behavior. Each time the child complies, you should reinforce their desired behavior. Over time, they will learn to respond repeatedly—and positively—to the timer. Eventually, you can slowly fade its use.

The ultimate win? The child becomes more independent, needing fewer reminders in the future. The behavior you foster is not just the act of teeth brushing but self-reliance.

2. Timers enhance prosocial behavior.

Timers help children build confidence. First, they teach children how to complete tasks in a given time. Second, they help children learn when to ask for assistance or direction. Third, they ease the tension some children feel when they start a new task. As a result, children feel more prepared, optimistic, and self-assured.

3. Timers reduce parent or educator stress.

One of the biggest challenges parents, educators, and caregivers face is knowing they might be seen as the "bad guy" when enforcing rules or transitions. Nobody enjoys being the constant enforcer or bearing the brunt of a child's frustration. Enter the timer—a neutral third party. It takes on the role of signaling a task's beginning or end. It directs the child's negative response away from the parent. Now, the adult can step in, not as an enforcer but as the bearer of reinforcement or rewards contingent upon the learner's responses to the timer.

4. Timers provide a neutrally preferred stimulus.

Since the timer is an impersonal device, it becomes a "neutrally preferred stimulus." That means that while it signals a task (which might be less preferred), it doesn't carry any emotional weight. The child will associate the task's aversiveness with the concept of time limits, not a person. The child learns to respond to the timer without associating negative emotions with the caregiver or educator.

5. Timers help children view their caregiver as a positive reinforcer.

When you use timers effectively, you position yourself as the deliverer of good news, rewards, and other reinforcements. The timer might signal the end of playtime, but YOU provide the treat, praise, or next enjoyable activity when the learner responds appropriately to the transition. That strengthens the positive association between you and your loved one or learners. You solidify your status as "the source of good things."

In short, timers streamline behavioral processes. They promote healthy habits, foster self-regulation, and build stronger relationships between children and adults. It's all about creating a structured, predictable environment where everyone knows the expectations and availability of reinforcers and how to get those desired outcomes.

APPLICATION
Timers in Action

Timers can be incredibly effective when implemented correctly. Let's look at real-life examples to see how they can fit seamlessly into the home and classroom. Remember, the golden rule here is to pair timers with reinforcement!

TIMERS IN THE HOME

BRUSHING TEETH

- "I'm setting the timer for one minute. During this time, I need you to keep your mouth open and let me brush your teeth. If you do well, you can choose tonight's bedtime story!"

This approach transforms a potentially challenging task into a game with a reward at the end.

MORNING ROUTINES:

- "We have seven minutes to get ready this morning. If you're all set by the time the timer goes off, you can watch TV for a few minutes before school!"

Here, the timer helps quicken a typically slow morning routine, with TV time as the enticement.

SIGNALING A BEHAVIORAL RESPONSE:

- "I'm setting this timer for three minutes; when the timer goes off, please change your shirt and put your shoes on. If you can do this without additional reminders or help from me, you can listen to your favorite song when we get in the car."

DISCUSSING SENSITIVE TOPICS WITH TEENAGERS:

- "I get that talking about some things can be tough. But let's chat for five minutes. If we can have a constructive conversation, you can invite your friend for a sleepover tonight."

This technique provides a safe, time-limited space for potentially challenging discussions, with the promise of some social time afterward.

SETTING REMINDERS FOR ROUTINE TASKS:

- If your loved one often forgets daily tasks like brushing teeth or taking medication, have them set a timer on their phone. When the timer rings, and they immediately do the task, reward them with a perk, like extra phone time or a pass on a usual chore.

Over time, this reinforcement reduces the need for reminders, encouraging independent behavior.

TIMERS IN THE CLASSROOM

FOR YOUNGER CHILDREN DURING CENTER TIME:

- "All right, friends, you have two more minutes of center time. When the timer goes off, start cleaning up. And if everyone tidies up nicely, we'll get five extra minutes at recess!"

Here, the timer acts as a neutral transition cue, and the extra recess time reinforces the desired behavior.

FOR ELEMENTARY-AGED CHILDREN DURING WORKSHEET TIME:

- "You have four more minutes to finish your worksheet. When the timer rings, put your pencils and worksheets away and wait for the next instruction. Those sitting quietly will get some free-choice time before our next activity."

This setup encourages timely task completion and smooth transitions, with free-choice time as the reward.

SIGNALING A BEHAVIORAL RESPONSE:

- "Class, when the timer goes off, I need everyone to turn their voice off, eyes on me, and pencils down so I can deliver the next set of instructions. If we can do this, there will be some free time before this class period ends."

Timers can be a potent tool, transitioning from one task to the next while keeping things upbeat. Additionally, timers can serve as reminder signals to prompt a desired and requested behavioral response. They also prevent you from being the "bad guy," constantly delivering non-preferred requests and removing valuable reinforcers. Instead, timers provide a neutral cue that's consistent and reliable. Remember to keep those reinforcements ready so you can encourage desired outcomes, especially at the outset!!

The Kapoor siblings found structure and even joy in their routine with the aid of a timer. They became more organized and self-reliant, thanks to Mrs. Emerson's great advice.

Likewise, your loved ones and learners can benefit from timers. We can all turn our daily challenges into harmonious routines with some innovation and understanding, making every household and classroom feel as whimsical as Brightville.

APPLICATION EXERCISE

Timers

INSTRUCTIONS

Harness the power of timers in your daily routine with this three-part exercise. Let's tackle three fun challenges to learn how to incorporate timers into your life.

1. Speedy Gonzalez Challenge

Objective: Improve the efficiency of specific tasks your child takes too long to complete.

Task: List three activities where you could use a timer to increase the speed of completion. Remember the morning routine example? Allow your child to access a special reinforcer if they complete the task before the timer rings.

TARGET ACTIVITY	CURRENT COMPLETION TIME	GOAL COMPLETION TIME	DATE OF ATTEMPT SUCCESSFUL? (Y OR N)
1.			
2.			
3.			

2. Smooth Transition Challenge

Objective: Use a timer to assist in transitioning your child away from highly preferred activities without challenging behaviors.

Task: Identify some activities your child loves so much that transitioning away might trigger resistance or challenging behaviors. How can you use a timer to signal the end of these activities? Think about transitioning from iPad time or playtime.

HIGHLY PREFERRED ACTIVITY TO TARGET FOR SMOOTH TRANSITION	REINFORCER I WILL OFFER FOR A SMOOTH TRANSITION	DATES OF ATTEMPT SUCCESSFUL? (Y OR N)
1.		
2.		
3.		

3. Targeting Tolerance

Objective: Employ the timer to increase your child's tolerance towards less-preferred or aversive activities.

Task: Think of activities where you can use a timer to indicate how long your child needs to engage or tolerate a task.

Remember, start with amounts of time much lower than the child can handle to establish success. Pair less-preferred activities with reinforcements and gradually increase the time to increase the child's tolerance to an aversive task. Activities can range from sitting at the dinner table and working on a tricky worksheet to standing still during teeth brushing. Using a timer for these activities provides a clear structure and makes these tasks less daunting.

LESS-PREFERRED OR AVERSIVE ACTIVITY	CURRENT TIME TOLERATED WITHOUT PROBLEM BEHAVIORS	TIME GOAL FOR TOLERANCE	POTENTIAL REINFORCERS CONTINGENT UPON APPROPRIATE TOLERANCE	DATES OF ATTEMPT SUCCESSFUL? (Y OR N)
1.				
2.				
3.				

Complete these exercises and see the transformative power of timers in action. Focus on clear communication, realistic expectations, and consistent reinforcement.

As partners in the pursuit of a Behavior Breakthrough, we NEVER bribe children!

BEHAVIORAL SKILL 12

Discriminating Bribes from Reinforcement

here was an enchanted sweets shop in Brightville called Whimsical Wonders. The candies there were not your everyday treats; they had truly unique qualities. Parents visited the store to buy candies that would help them manage their children's behavior. A wise older woman named Elara ran the shop.

One bright morning, Mrs. Wilson and Mr. Schein, two parents from Brightville, entered the shop, each with their young ones in tow. Mrs. Wilson's foster daughter, Clara, was sweet but notoriously restless and fidgety. Mr. Shein's son, Evan, was known to throw tantrums at the drop of a hat.

"I need something to help Clara sit still during our family dinners," Mrs. Wilson lamented.

"And I need something to stop Evan's outbursts," Mr. Shein added.

With her keen eyes, Elara could see each parent's

challenges. She handed Mrs. Wilson a shimmering blue candy called "Pacify Pops." She gave Mr. Shein a sparkling red one called "Tranquil Treats."

"Remember," Elara warned, "these candies are special. One reinforces behavior, while the other stops behavior. But misuse them, and they might not encourage what you truly desire."

Eager to enjoy a peaceful meal, Mrs. Wilson immediately handed Clara the "Pacify Pop" that evening when she wouldn't sit still. The candy worked wonders, and Clara immediately settled down. Meanwhile, Mr. Shein gave Evan the "Tranquil Treat" every time he launched into a tantrum, instantly pacifying him.

After a few days, Amelia Wilson and Jack Schein returned to Whimsical Wonders, still frustrated and with different tales to tell.

"Clara only quietly sits if I give her a candy," Amelia sighed. She added that Clara had also started becoming louder and more restless in hopes of receiving the candy in other situations.

Jack echoed, "Evan stops his tantrums when he sees the candy, but he's been having them more frequently."

Elara nodded knowingly, "Ah, Mrs. Wilson, you've been using the candy as a bribe. You're offering it after the undesired behavior has started. And Mr. Shein, you've been reinforcing Evan's tantrums. He has learned he'll get a treat if he starts acting up."

The parents exchanged embarrassed glances. They hadn't used the candies wisely.

Elara continued, "Mrs. Wilson, try offering Clara the Pacify Pop before dinner, telling her it's a treat for those who sit calmly during meals. She can only be awarded after she sits still. And Jack, reward Evan with the Tranquil Treat after periods where he's behaved well, not after he throws tantrums."

Both parents heeded Elara's advice. Mrs. Wilson started to offer Clara the candy before meals and praised her for sitting calmly. Whenever she sat calmly and ate her food, Clara got the candy. Before long, Clara began associating the treat with desired behavior—sitting peacefully—so she began to do it without her mother even mentioning the candy.

Mr. Shein, too, started rewarding Evan after he'd exhibited prosocial behavior for extended periods rather than during his tantrums. Evan began to understand that desired behavior yielded sweet results.

As weeks turned into months, the need for the enchanted candies diminished. Clara and Evan had internalized their desired behaviors and no longer expected treats for every prosocial choice.

Mrs. Wilson and Mr. Shein returned to Elara's shop, not for candies but to thank her. Elara smiled and said, "Remember, it's not about stopping a behavior momentarily, but about nurturing the right habits in the long run."

And so, the parents of Brightville learned an important lesson on the difference between a bribe and a reinforcer. The tale of the enchanted candies became a legend, a study in parenting passed down through generations.

And Brightville? It became a town where children grew up understanding the value of prosocial behaviors, all thanks to the wisdom of Mrs. Emerson, the families who heeded her advice, and yes, also Elara and her Whimsical Wonders.

We're almost at the end! We've come so far, and you've learned so much. In this final behavioral skill, we'll explore the contrasts between a bribe and reinforcement and why it matters so much to understand their differences.

You may have wondered: "Shouldn't my child make the right choices simply because that's the expectation?" In a perfect world, yes. But in the real world, sometimes that isn't enough. But bribes aren't the answer either, and they usually just make things worse. Yet, our culture often equates reinforcement with bribes, thinking either option will get children to behave better. Nothing could be further from the truth! Let's learn why by digging into some important differences.

ESSENTIALS
Bribes vs. Reinforcement

It's crucial to understand the distinction between bribes and reinforcement if you want truly effective behavioral management. To break it down:

- **Reinforcement** offers a desirable or preferred outcome BEFORE the behavior begins. The goal is to INCREASE the likelihood of a desired behavior being repeated.

- **Bribes** offer a desirable outcome AFTER the onset of undesired behaviors, intending to stop them. This action inadvertently reinforces the undesired behavior.

With bribes, there is a predictable chain of events: Problematic Behavior → Offer of a Reward → Cessation of the Problematic Behavior → Receipt of Preferred Outcome.

This pattern reinforces the idea that problematic behavior must occur to receive the desired outcome. The sequence matters because it dictates what behavior or chain of behaviors you are reinforcing.

By contrast, reinforcement sets the stage for desired behavior by offering the child a reward before the behavior begins. In many cases, the need for external reinforcement may be temporary. At some point, the child will likely embrace the notion of desired behavior simply because it produces such a wide range of preferred results. In the meantime, you can use reinforcements to increase the child's tolerance, teach new skills, and help the child display prosocial behavior, even ones that may not occur naturally in the environment!

Does this distinction really matter? *Yes!* Bribes unintentionally encourage children to act out *more*, especially if a child knows that a reward might follow an outburst. Reinforcement, however, celebrates healthy choices and encourages children to display desired behavior without falling back into old habits or challenging behaviors.

We also need to deal with a common misconception—one I always hear. Many parents and educators ask,

"Why should I have to use reinforcement? All the other children are doing what they are supposed to do. Shouldn't my child/learner be expected to behave themselves, too? Why should I give them a reward to get them to do what other kids are already doing?"

Consider this: There are many reasons why children misbehave, including aversiveness, difficulty, or sheer opposition to the parent or teacher. In these instances, the child has no "intrinsic" motivation to behave appropriately; they do not feel an internal desire to comply. Additionally, there may be environmental factors that influence their decision to act out (sensory overload is one example). Reinforcement reminds the child that rewards are contingent on correct responses.

External reinforcement steps in and serves as a jump-start to motivate prosocial behavior.

Think about the first time a child says "mama." The jubilation, the applause, and the celebration are all external reinforcers to ensure that the child repeats the behavior. Similarly, throughout life, we benefit from moments of external encouragement and validation, even for tasks we're expected to do. When a manager recognizes an employee for their hard work or a friend praises their trusted friend for always being there, these acknowledgments are powerful. They not only validate the behavior but motivate its *continuation*.

Reinforcement isn't just about rewarding "extraordinary" actions; it recognizes and nurtures desired behaviors, ensuring they become a natural part of someone's routine.

Rather than seeing reinforcement as an unnecessary indulgence, view it as an essential tool to shape and guide behaviors for the better.

Remember, everyone is different. We have varied preferences and needs. Therefore, it's no surprise that people respond differently to expectations. If your child or learner needs reinforcement to learn a skill, display prosocial behavior, or tolerate something aversive, it's your job to provide it! It's not bribing; it's meeting an individual's needs.

REASONING
The Nuances of Bribing

When differentiating between bribery and reinforcement, consider the *timing* of the preferred outcome. If you present a child with a preferred outcome to encourage desired behavior BEFORE they act out, that's a reinforcement plan. If you promise, offer, or even mention the future availability of something good AFTER they've started acting out in the hopes they will stop, that's a bribe.

In certain situations, offering a bribe may seem necessary. But it's essential to recognize the long-term impact on behavior. Reinforcers strategically foster desired behaviors, whereas bribes unintentionally promote undesired behavior. Here are some examples of bribery in everyday situations we can likely all relate to:

1. **Preschool Setting:** A child refuses to sit during carpet time, running around instead. By offering a book to entice them to sit down *after* misbehaving, you are bribing them.

2. **Shopping Scenario:** A child throws a tantrum because they want a toy. If you say, "Stop crying, and we might look at it again," *after* the tantrum starts, you are offering a bribe.

3. **Restaurant Situation:** A child misbehaves while waiting for food. Offering phone time to behave *after* they've been disruptive is a bribe.

4. **Recess Trouble:** A child refuses to line up after recess is over. By offering the child time in the sensory corner for compliance *after* they've been defiant, you are bribing them.

5. **Teenager's Phone:** A teen refuses to hand over their phone for a check. Offering a shopping trip in exchange for the phone *after* the initial refusal is a bribe.

6. **Classwork:** A student fails to turn in assignments. Offering to drop their lowest grades in exchange for completion *after* the fact is a bribe.

Hopefully, these examples help you recognize the patterns in your responses and the behaviors they might inadvertently encourage. Bribery can be tempting. But stop and consider the long-term repercussions. To solidify your understanding, let's apply the three-term ABC contingency explored in previous chapters (antecedent, behavior, and consequence):

Scenario: You tell a child it's bedtime (antecedent). The child starts crying, not wanting to go to bed (behavior). You then promise them an extra story if they go to bed quietly (consequence).

Question: Is this a bribe or reinforcement?

Answer: It's a bribe because the offer of an extra story came AFTER the undesired behavior (crying).

While there may be situations where a bribe feels like the only option, understanding the distinction and long-term effects ensures that you can make informed decisions for the best outcomes. To avoid bribing your child, offer preferred outcomes only AFTER they demonstrate the desired behavior—no exceptions!

APPLICATION
Bribe vs. Reinforcer Quiz

Ready to fine-tune your radar? I want you to answer this question: "Is it a bribe or reinforcer?" Below are a few relatable scenarios and a question after each. To maximize the impact, let's review the three-term ABC contingency, which is an essential concept in understanding behavior.

- Antecedent: What happens *before* the behavior
- Behavior: The observed action or reaction
- Consequence: What *follows* the behavior, which can either reinforce or deter the behavior in the future

Analyze each scenario and determine whether the consequence offered acts as a bribe (offered *after* the onset of undesired behavior) or as a reinforcer (offered *before* undesired behavior in hopes that it will increase the likelihood of a desired behavior being repeated).

EXAMPLE 1

- A (Antecedent): It's homework time, and the task is challenging.

- B (Behavior): The child begins to cry and throw a tantrum.
- C (Consequence): The parent says, "If you stop crying and finish your homework, you can have an extra 30 minutes of TV time."

Question: Is the consequence a bribe or a reinforcer? If the consequence is a bribe, what can you do instead to prevent problematic behaviors in the future?

EXAMPLE 2

- A (Antecedent): A child is learning to tie their shoes.
- B (Behavior): The child successfully ties their shoe for the first time.
- C (Consequence): The parent gives praise and a high-five.

Question: Is the consequence a bribe or a reinforcer? If the consequence is a bribe, what can you do instead to prevent problematic behaviors in the future?

EXAMPLE 3

- A (Antecedent): The teacher announces that whoever finishes their classwork first can choose a book for storytime.
- B (Behavior): A student works diligently and finishes first.
- C (Consequence): The student gets to choose the book for storytime.

Question: Is the consequence a bribe or a reinforcer? If the consequence is a bribe, what can you do instead to prevent problematic behaviors in the future?

EXAMPLE 4

- A (Antecedent): It's bedtime, and the child doesn't want to go to sleep.
- B (Behavior): The child screams and refuses to lie down.
- C (Consequence): The parent says, "If you lie down quietly for ten minutes, I'll read you an extra story."

Question: Is the consequence a bribe or a reinforcer? If the consequence is a bribe, what can you do instead to prevent problematic behaviors in the future?

EXAMPLE 5

- A (Antecedent): It's time for the family to leave the park.
- B (Behavior): The child quickly gathers their toys and heads to the car without being asked.
- C (Consequence): The parent says, "Since you were so helpful, let's get ice cream on the way home."

Question: Is the consequence a bribe or a reinforcer? If the consequence is a bribe, what can you do instead to prevent problematic behaviors in the future?

In our daily lives, we too face situations where we must decide how to motivate or guide behavior, be it our own behavior or that of our loved ones, students, or colleagues. The distinction between bribes and reinforcement isn't merely a play of words; it's about the timing, intention, and long-term effects on behavior and character development.

As the citizens of Brightville learned each new behavior skill, they realized that their approach to behavior, motivation, and reward is never as black and white as it may seem. Every action, consequence, and incentive carries a deeper meaning that requires understanding and reflection.

As you step out of Brightville and into the real world, remember its lessons. Seek to understand the WHY behind behaviors. Aim to guide, not control. And always remember that the power lies not in the reward itself but in its ability to foster genuine motivation and desired change.

APPLICATION EXERCISE

Distinguishing Bribes from Reinforcers

PURPOSE

This exercise will help you further differentiate between bribes and reinforcement by analyzing various scenarios. By the end, you should be able to identify when a behavior-contingent reward is being used proactively (reinforcement) versus a reactive reward (bribe). You should consider the implications of each.

INSTRUCTIONS

1. **Scenario Analysis:** Below are various scenarios. For each one, decide whether it's an example of a bribe or reinforcement. Note your answers.

2. **Reflection:** After identifying each scenario, reflect on why you categorized it as such. What are the implications of using a bribe versus reinforcement?

3. **Role-play (optional):** Pair up with a friend. Take turns acting out different scenarios. One will offer a bribe or reinforcement, and the other will respond. That will give both participants a sense of how each option feels.

SCENARIOS

- **Scenario 1:** Your child throws a tantrum in the store because they want a toy. You promise them the toy if they stop crying and behave for the rest of the shopping trip.

- **Scenario 2:** You tell your child that if they finish their homework every day this week without complaint, they can choose a movie for family movie night on Friday.

- **Scenario 3:** Your student hesitates to take on a new project. You offer extra time on the iPad if they agree to do it right away.

- **Scenario 4:** Before starting a difficult lesson, a teacher tells her students that those who actively participate and try their best will get an extra ten minutes of recess.

- **Scenario 5:** Your child begins to raise their voice and argue. You quickly promise them a treat if they stop and speak calmly.

- **Scenario 6:** At the beginning of the month, you set a goal with your basketball team that if they meet the target, there will be a team outing at the end of the month.

REFLECTION QUESTIONS

1. In which scenarios did the reward come before the behavior spiraled out of control?

2. How might the outcome or feeling differ for the individual receiving a bribe versus reinforcement?

3. Can you think of a situation where you inadvertently bribed someone instead of using reinforcement? How might you handle it differently now?

By actively working through these scenarios and reflecting on the outcomes, you will better understand the nuances between bribes and reinforcement. The goal is not to give you "busy work" but to help you make more informed decisions in real-life situations.

PART III

INTEGRATING
STRATEGIES FOR A
BRIGHTER FUTURE

Welcome to the final stretch! You've read tales from Brightville, absorbed the wisdom of Mrs. Emerson, and familiarized yourself with these new skills for guiding behavior. It's time to weave everything into a cohesive, actionable plan.

You're about to see all you've learned distilled into eight essential steps to achieve reinforcement mastery. Think of it as your blueprint to breakthrough!

Focus on refining, consolidating, and mastering your approach. The tools you'll gather will empower you to reshape environments and create lasting, beneficial change.

YOUR JOURNEY FORWARD

Eight Steps
to Reinforcement Mastery

ears passed in Brightville, and the tales of Mrs. Emerson's arrival became legendary. Parents and educators who once faced so many challenging behaviors now found themselves empowered, applying each of Mrs. Emerson's twelve behavioral skills—all in the proper order.

The people of Brightville now stood tall, their hope revived and hearts full of optimism. *Descriptive praise* uplifted their spirits, and *directed choices* enabled them to act with agency. The magic of *timers* brought structure. Indeed, each skill wove its unique thread into the fabric of the town.

Those who experienced behavior breakthroughs in Brightville learned to observe rather than merely see. Each day, they became more aware of the needs and desires of their loved ones and learners. They saw the importance of *stating things positively*, the power of *addressing denials*, and the beauty of *being aware of behavioral functions*. They realized that the environment in which they raised their children was as pivotal as the values they instilled.

Parents became masters at *delivering preferred outcomes*, celebrating achievements by offering outcomes they knew their loved ones enjoyed.

Following the wisdom of Mrs. Emerson, educators became sculptors of young minds. Classrooms were no longer zones of frustrated instruction; instead, they transformed into places of growth and discovery. Powerful *reinforcement* tools, such as *first/then contingencies* and *preferred outcomes*, created harmonious learning experiences wherever they were employed. *Antecedent expectations* also made it easier for students to engage in their tasks.

Yet, of all the behavioral skills, the *discrimination between bribes and reinforcement* stood out as a beacon, guiding the people of Brightville to nurture intrinsic motivation and a genuine love for growth.

The learners, filled with newfound confidence and resilience, became the pride of Brightville. The tales of their successes were shared far and wide, bringing hope to towns beyond their own.

As the sun set on another glorious day, families gathered in the town square. A community once lost in shadows found its light. Brightville had become a testament to the power of reinforcement. And while every day had its own story, one thing remained constant: they all learned and loved harmoniously forever after.

The Brightville stories might seem like whimsical narrations from a make-believe place. Nothing is perfect; "happily ever after" requires honest and ongoing work, and success is never guaranteed. But the town's essence is rooted in the realities you and I navigate daily. Brightville mirrors the experiences of loved ones and learners everywhere, and the strategies Mrs. Emerson introduced resonate with the tools we can employ in our homes, schools, and communities.

Now, as we transition from the streets of Brightville to the days and weeks that lie ahead, let's gather our thoughts and chart a course forward. The goal, as always, is to bring about transformation, one strategy at a time.

We've discussed the complexities and nuances of behavior change. As we solidify our understanding, remember that tangible change comes from implementing these behavioral skills seamlessly into your daily life. It's about making them second nature, like driving a car or riding a bike.

I can't do that for you—that's a step you alone must take. But as we draw to a close, I can provide a few steps that will offer additional context and practical application. Understanding these principles isn't enough; you must wield them effectively. Here is a list of the actionable skill sets to develop as you record data, monitor your progress, adjust your approach, deliver reinforcement, and keep forging ahead!

1. Develop fluency in prevention strategies.

While it's vital to understand the twelve behavioral skills, it's equally crucial to apply them. Like learning a new language, these strategies require practice until they become a natural part of your behavioral interactions.

Context: Imagine learning a new language. Initially, you might stumble through the words, but with practice, the words flow effortlessly off your tongue. These new skills may not feel comfortable at first. That's normal! Practice them until they become second nature.

Application: Start small. Take the first strategy (descriptive praise) and set a clear goal. Commit to using it consistently for three consecutive days. Make it a conscious effort throughout your day. Practice refines your skills until they're automatic.

CHALLENGE:
THE THREE-DAY FLUENCY BOOTCAMP

For the next three days, think of yourself as a student at the Prevention Strategies Language School. Each day, focus solely on the first strategy: descriptive praise. Create a mini-journal or use sticky notes to record every time you successfully apply it. Celebrate those little wins! By the end of Day 3, reflect on your journey, noting the changes in your ease of application. Are you ready to make this strategy a fluent part of your language?

2. Confidently determine function.

Deciphering the reasons behind certain behaviors is pivotal. Without knowing what environmental variables are maintaining the behavior, you merely address symptoms, not the underlying problem. You don't want to play a guessing game with behaviors. You want to be methodical and *effective*.

Context: Attempting behavior change without understanding its underlying purpose is like trying to hit a bullseye blindfolded. Data collection is your sight; it reveals the target.

Application: Channel your inner detective. Pay close attention to antecedents (what happens *before* a behavior) and consequences (what *follows* the behavior). Remember, patterns emerge over time, so document your observations. For example, suppose you see a pattern of consequences that attention (the function), and you determine that pattern is driving the undesired behavior. When you see problematic behavior, you must give your child the attention they seek less frequently.

That's not the natural response. In fact, this is an especially difficult choice since it goes against the parental instincts that push us to approach, correct, and problem-solve. However, once you experience your own behavior breakthrough, you should understand the functions of behavior and seek to make changes that encourage prosocial behaviors while delivering that sought-after attention at the right time.

> **BONUS INSIGHT:**
> **CULTURE MAY CLOUD YOUR ASSESSMENT**
>
> Did you know that our culture conditions us to react to behaviors in a certain way? Sometimes, these conditioned reactions can be counterproductive. Instead of going with what feels instinctual, adopt a more analytical approach, using data to guide your decisions.

3. Know when to seek help.

Let's normalize seeking help when we need it! If behaviors escalate to a level where they're harmful or you feel overwhelmed, it's time to consult the professionals. Seeking help is not a sign of weakness; it's a sign of strength. It shows that you understand your limits.

Context: Imagine you're climbing a steep mountain. Most people would seek a guide's expertise if the path becomes treacherous or the summit seems elusive. Similarly, complex behaviors often require professional guidance.

Application: Recognize the signs. If behaviors pose physical harm, threaten safety, or routinely leave you feeling helpless, it's time to consult experts. Seek assistance from professionals like mental health therapists, behavior analysts, and pediatricians. Collaboration is a strength, not a weakness.

CASE STUDY: TALK TO A FRIEND

Talk to a friend who has previously sought professional help for a child. Ask how that process went and what improved after a professional got involved. What would that friend have changed about the process? What were they most pleased with about the process?

4. Find a reinforcement that fits the bill.

Once you understand a behavior's function, it's time to apply the right type of reinforcement. Think of this as finding the right key to a lock; it has to fit perfectly for the desired outcome.

Context: Reinforcement is the currency of behavior change. Just as you pay for a service, the reinforcement must match the behavior's function precisely.

Application: Tailor your reinforcement strategy. If it's escape the child is after, offer a break from the aversive task contingent upon their display of desired behaviors or when the learner appropriately requests a break—*before* the undesired behavior occurs. For attention-seekers, provide quality interaction contingent upon displays of desired behaviors or when the learner appropriately requests an interaction. Ensure your "payment" aligns with the service rendered (the desired behavior).

5. Teach effective replacement behaviors.

This process is not just about curbing unwanted behaviors but instilling desired ones. Think of it as removing weeds and planting flowers. By teaching effective replacement behaviors, you're providing the tools necessary for individuals to respond appropriately in situations where they previously might have struggled. It's akin to equipping someone with a map and compass in a previously uncharted territory.

Context: Picture this as upgrading from an old, inefficient system to a new, streamlined one. The replacement behavior should serve the same function as the problem behavior but in a more beneficial manner.

Application: Identify the function of the problem behavior. If the child seeks sensory stimulation, teach them to ask for a sensory break. For attention-seekers, help them to learn how to initiate a conversation politely. Think of it like installing an updated, user-friendly app.

6. Employ immediate reinforcement for prosocial behavior.

Once you observe a desired behavior, it's essential to reinforce it immediately, especially during the initial stages. That is where a behavior-reinforcement chart will come in handy.

Context: Consider this like training a new employee. Immediate praise for correctly doing their job reinforces the desired actions and ensures a clear connection between proper actions and rewards.

Application: Timing is crucial. When the child exhibits desired behaviors, respond promptly with the appropriate reinforcement (one that aligns with the function of behavior). Immediate rewards reinforce the behavior's value and likelihood of recurrence.

7. Master the art of fading reinforcement.

While immediate and consistent reinforcement is initially essential, the goal is to reduce external rewards over time, leading to intrinsic motivation.

Context: Think of fading reinforcement as gradually transitioning from training wheels to a two-wheeler. You want to reduce reliance on external rewards while increasing independence.

Application: As the replacement behaviors become consistent, gradually lessen the immediacy, frequency, and amount of reinforcement. Increase tolerance and self-sufficiency. Picture teaching a child to swim; initially, they need floaties, then a kickboard, then a noodle, then doggie paddling. Over time, they swim independently.

PRACTICAL EXAMPLE:
WATCH AS GOOD HABITS FORM

A child who initially receives praise every time they put away toys might start receiving occasional rewards, then praise every few times. Finally, the behavior becomes a habit without needing any reinforcement.

---

8. Evaluate and repeat.

Behavioral interventions aren't a one-time solution. You must commit to assessing their effectiveness and adjust strategies as needed. If an old problematic behavior resurfaces, it's an indicator to reevaluate and start the cycle again. But never fear—as long as you have identified the function of the behavior correctly, the cycle is much shorter when repeated.

Context: The journey of reinforcing desired behaviors is much like tending to a garden; it requires patience, observation, and sometimes a change in tactics when old challenges sprout up again.

Application: Schedule regular self-check-ins (or check-ins with your team if you're a professional) to review the behavioral skills you've implemented. Make a note of what's working and what's not. Don't be discouraged if a specific behavior has improved but later regresses. Instead, view it as an opportunity to refine your approach. Perhaps the environment has changed. Dive back into the strategies, revisit the lessons from Brightville, and adjust your methods. It's a continuous cycle of learning and adapting, with every challenge as an opportunity for growth.

ACTIVITY: SCHEDULE REFLECTION TIME

At the end of every month, reflect on the behaviors observed, the behavioral skills implemented, and their effectiveness. Adjust your approach based on this reflection.

Your Breakthrough is Waiting!

We've reached the end, and I know—it's a lot. But here's the good (great!) news. Your efforts will lead to a remarkable transformation when your loved one or learner becomes intrinsically motivated to display desired behaviors.

Setbacks are part of the process, so expect them. And if problem behaviors resurface, don't lose hope. Simply revisit these fundamental steps and start anew. Reevaluate behavioral function and what is potentially reinforcing the resurfaced problem behavior. Ultimately, this path paves the way for genuine and lasting behavior change, empowering you to be a true transformation agent!

Every human is unique. And our needs change daily (and even multiple times daily) depending on environmental variables. Tailor your approach, stay adaptable, and continue to learn and grow alongside your children, students, and colleagues.

As we reach the end of our journey through Brightville and Mrs. Emerson's behavioral skills, there's a big takeaway: *Understanding behavior is everything, and every person is unique.* When your loved one or learner acts out or does something unexpected, they're often just trying to use the environment to meet their needs.

So, don't base your actions or responses on gut feelings or what you read on random blogs. Instead, keep track of what's happening. Spot patterns. What sets off certain behaviors? What rewards do they get? When you get those answers, you can start making beneficial changes.

If things get tricky or a bit much, it's okay to ask for help. No one's expecting you to be a knight in shining armor. There are loads of experts, from therapists to school counselors to pediatricians, who can lend a hand.

Behavior is like a puzzle you can piece together with patience, understanding, and one evidence-based strategy after another. And if you ever get stuck? Just think back to Brightville and remember that sometimes, someone just needs a little nudge in the right direction.

Thanks for being willing to learn with me as you seek breakthroughs for your loved ones and learners. Let's keep making the world brighter, one behavioral skill at a time!

ABOUT THE AUTHORS

About Bailey

Bailey Payne, MS, BCBA, LBA, is a wife to Aaron, a girl mama to Renley and Pearson, and a full-time board-certified behavior analyst. Her passion is serving humans with quality, evidence-based interventions that maximize potential. She LOVES watching people smash goals!

Bailey was raised in rural Kansas (with dirt roads and no stoplights). That upbringing solidified her commitment later in life to bringing research, services, and information to the underserved in rural areas. Since she was a little girl, Bailey connected with humans who displayed exceptionalities, including developing friendships with children who used wheelchairs for mobility, used sign language to communicate, and experienced other special traits. Her early love for those with unique traits seemed innate and natural, and thus, she devoted her life and career to serving people and their loved ones to promote independence and a higher quality of life. Bailey feels so lucky to do what she does because every family she serves fills her up and brings her so much joy!

She has a master's degree in clinical psychology from Pittsburg State University in Kansas. Bailey's professional experience includes working as a psychologist at a state hospital, an autism specialist for the Kansas Autism Waiver, a project therapist with the University of Kansas Lifespan Institute, a behavioral specialist with The May Institute of Autism, and a licensed behavior analyst serving the Bowling Green, Kentucky community.

About Jen

Jen is honored to co-author *Behavior Breakthrough* alongside Bailey, a distinguished BCBA and expert in the field. Initially joining as a ghostwriter, Bailey's recognition of collaborative effort brought Jen to the forefront. Jen is passionate about bringing influential ideas to life through words, and she has ghostwritten over 50 books, helping thought leaders and influencers share their knowledge and stories. She loves her job because it allows her to learn about diverse subjects and interact with professionals who are the best at what they do!

Beyond Jen's professional pursuits, she is a dedicated homeschool mom to three wonderful boys (Porter, Wyatt, and Jesse) and a proud wife to Will. Balancing the roles of an author and educator at home, Jen thrives on the rich experiences that her professional and personal lives offer. You can find Jen on a given day walking on her under-desk treadmill as she works amidst the chaos of life with three boys and juggles unscheduled visits from the neighbors (her parents).

Behavior Breakthrough makes a great gift for the holidays and other special occasions! If you're interested in a bulk discount, head to our site and click on our store:
BaileyPayne.com

Want a downloadable version of any of the exercises or charts you saw in this book, or want to stay up to date with our new programs and help videos? Visit us at:
BaileyPayne.com/Breakthrough

A free ebook edition is available with the purchase of this book.

To claim your free ebook edition:

1. Visit MorganJamesBOGO.com
2. Sign your name CLEARLY in the space
3. Complete the form and submit a photo of the entire copyright page
4. You or your friend can download the ebook to your preferred device

Morgan James BOGO™

A **FREE** ebook edition is available for you or a friend with the purchase of this print book.

CLEARLY SIGN YOUR NAME ABOVE

Instructions to claim your free ebook edition:
1. Visit MorganJamesBOGO.com
2. Sign your name CLEARLY in the space above
3. Complete the form and submit a photo of this entire page
4. You or your friend can download the ebook to your preferred device

Print & Digital Together Forever.

Snap a photo

Free ebook

Read anywhere

Printed in the USA
CPSIA information can be obtained
at www.ICGtesting.com
JSHW011059021124
72776JS00003B/5